JAPANESE PAPER DOLLS

Shimotsuke Hitogata

**by Shigeo
and Shizuko
Suwa**

SHUFUNOTOMO CO., LTD.
TOKYO, JAPAN

7th printing, 1990

All rights reserved throughout the world.
No part of this book may be reproduced in any form
without permission in writing from the publisher.

© Copyright in Japan 1976 by Shigeo and Shizuko Suwa
Translated from the original Japanese edition by Cheryl Ando
Illustrations by Ran Kanai

Published by SHUFUNOTOMO CO., LTD.
2-9, Kanda Surugadai, Chiyoda-ku, Tokyo, 101 Japan

ISBN 4-07-975380-2
Printed in Japan

PREFACE

Shimotsuke paper dolls are dolls made of paper by a traditional method of the *Shimotsuke* area (now *Tochigi* Prefecture). It has a beauty which makes one feel the simple gentility and sorrow that have been handed down in old legends and traditions. It is kind of doll anyone would love. The *Shimotsuke* gathered paper, traditional hand-gathered paper, is used. It is gathered piece by piece. This increases the softness and makes the most of the characteristics of paper. It is easy for anyone to use.

In this book we have explained everything so that it is easy to understand, especially for beginners. We explained how to make the head, body, clothes, hairstyles, miniature items and hair ornaments, in that order. In this one book we explained in detail through sketches and photographs the points of the basic process necessary to make all kinds of dolls.

We wrote down the estimated size as the standard size. This may be changed according to the size of the hand of the person making it. Make it freely without worrying about the size. Enjoy making something by hand!

Finally, we, the Suwa family, would like more people to know the enjoyment of making dolls. We want to hand down the Japanese traditions. Presented on the back cover is *Kannon* (The Goddess of Mercy) in our hope for peace.

諏訪重雄
Shigeo Suwa

諏訪志津子
Shizuko Suwa

CONTENTS

Facts about Paper 6
To Beginners 7
Basic *Shimotsuke* Doll Method 8

Spring Garden 9
Hina Dolls 10
Young *Samurai* 10
Dwarf 11
Suihatsu Style 12
Marumage Chignon 13
Taka-shimada 14
Shimada Chignon 14
Momoware Chignon 15
Traveling *Oiran* 15
Tachi-hyogo 16

Basic Point 1   HOW TO MAKE THE HEAD 17
   (1)   The Basic Short Bob 17
   (2)   Three Year-Old Boy's Head 19
   (3)   Adult's Head 19
   (4)   Various Standard Head Sizes 20

Basic Point 2   HOW TO MAKE THE BODY 21
   (1)   Child's Body (Basic Model) 21
      (a)   Torso padding and legs 21
      (b)   Breast 22
       *   Tips for Beginners 24
   (2)   Little Boy's Body 25
   (3)   Adult's Body 25
      (a)   Breast 26
      (b)   Hips 27
      (c)   Calves 28
   (4)   Body Model 28

Basic Point 3   *KIMONO* 29
   (1)   Child's *Kimono* 29
      (a)   *Kimono* 29
      (b)   *Obi* 31
   (2)   Adult's *Kimono* 33
      (a)   *Kimono* 33
   (3)   Adult's *Obi* 34
        Sageobi 34
        Hosoobi 35
        Taiko Obi 36
        Oiran Obi 37

Basic Point 4   HOW TO GATHER PAPER 38
      *   Various Kinds of Knot 39

Basic Point 5   HAIR STYLE 40
   (1)   Wigs 40

	(a)	Basic Short Bob Style	40
	*	Variations of the Short Bob—put on a chignon	42
		Variation 1 Bow	42
		Variation 2 The *Chigo* topknot	42
		Variation 3 The *Momoware*	43
		Variation 4 Boy Doll's Style	43
	(b)	Three Year-Old Boy	44
	(c)	The *Suihatsu* Style	44
(2)	Tied Up Hair Styles		46
	(a)	Woman's Hairdo	46
		Base of the tied up style	46
	*	Variations of the Adult's Hair	47
		Tachi-hyogo	47
		Shimada Chignon	48
		Taka-shimada	48
		Momoware	50
		Marumage	50
		Oiran Style	50
	(b)	Child's Hair Style	51
		Chigo-mage	51
		Kamuro	52
	(c)	Men's Styles	53
		Samurai's Topknot	53

Basic Point 6   **HOW TO MAKE THE MINIATURE ITEMS** .. 55

Decorative String 55
Combs 56
Tassels 56
Ornamental Hairpins 57
Flowers 58
Fringed Hairpins 58
Bells 59
Hakama 60
Hand-lamps 62
Doll-stand 63
Screen 64
Scepter 65
Swords 66
Dwarf's Bowl 68
Face-guard 69
Hair Ornaments 70
    Flat Hairpin 71
    Comb and Broad Hairpin 1 72
    Comb and Broad Hairpin 2 73
    Comb and Broad Hairpin 3 74
    Comb and Broad Hairpin 4 74
    Comb and Fringed Hairpin with Plum Blossoms .. 75
    Broad and Narrow Floral Hairpins 76
Dolls with Arms and Legs 77
Stands 78
Crown 80
Necklace 80

FACTS ABOUT PAPER
Getting to Know the Nature of Paper

Some of you will say you will not be good at this. Whether you will be good at this or not is only a matter of opinion. Anyone can make a beautiful doll if they understand the nature of paper, pay attention to details and make it carefully. After having had something to do with work involving paper over a long period of time, after handling paper and living with it, the paper will naturally convey its nature to you. You too will feel you are communicating with it.

Now, let's talk about the qualities, the nature of paper to prepare you for when you actually make the doll. The nature of paper is as complicated as that of a person. It has many aspects, such as its strength when made wet, its degree of expansion and contraction when glue is applied, how much it will spread or expand when two pieces are glued together, the direction it is easiest to bend in, tips on how to make it keep its shape, etc. Much effort over a long period of time is necessary before one can understand the complex qualities, the nature of paper by just looking at it. One cannot become an expert easily, so we will teach you only the basic important points.

The Grain of Paper

One of the basic points in the nature of paper is the lengthwise and widthwise grain. Just as a person's chest hurts when it is forcibly twisted, paper is strained when folded against the grain. All paper, whether it is Japanese or Western, has a grain. When paper has edges like that of Japanese paper, it is easy to know the direction of the grain. When it is cut in small pieces, it is difficult to know just by looking. You can find out by the following two methods. Try them with some paper you have at hand.

1. Wet the paper. When wet it will shrink and curl. The sides that curl up indicate the widthwise grain. The direction perpendicular to that is the lengthwise grain.

How to find out the direction of the grain by wetting the paper.

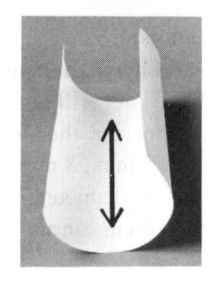

2. Fold the paper. The direction in which the paper can be easily folded with the fingertips is the lengthwise grain. The direction in which a little resistance can be felt when folded is the widthwise grain. As you can see, the paper stretches along the lengthwise grain and shrinks along the other. If you make the most of this knowledge when making something, the shape will not be distorted.

This is especially important when gluing two pieces of paper together. If you place them so the lengthwise grain of one piece crosses that of the other, their power to expand or contract will be the same. It will not warp, and the shape will not be distorted. If you do not do this, the flaps will bend back as shown in the above picture.

Keep the importance of the grain in mind as you make some things, and you will come to understand it naturally. Expect to make at least one that will not turn out well.

Incidentally, this is true about all things. If you come in contact with people, objects, nature and all things with a warm heart, you will be able to understand them and, in its turn, understand the nature of paper. Then, as you come to care about the nature of all things you can say you will be able to do your best. Now go ahead and try to make something.

*The drawing paper used for the backing is thicker than Japanese paper. If you mistake the direction of the grain, it will effect the finished product. So we have indicated the direction of the lengthwise grain with arrows in the sketches. When two pieces glued together are used for the backing, we have shown the lengthwise grains respectively with crossed arrows.

Cut the paper along the lengthwise grain. Japanese gathered paper has many small wrinkles, so do not worry about the grain direction very much at first. After you get used to it, use the same grain direction as the drawing paper.

TO BEGINNERS

For those of you who are coming into contact with Japanese paper dolls for the first time, we will now show you the necessary tools and materials.

Tools:
  *The gathering sticks (1)
    They will mainly be used for gathering paper or for the doll's coifure. They should be 5 mm., 8 mm., 1.1 cm., 1.4 cm., and 1.7 cm. in diameter. Those of you who do not have them can use pencils.

*Scissors (2)
*Wood-workers' glue (3)
  Use the white wood-workers' glue. It dries quickly and become transparent, so it is the best to use with paper.
*Damp towel (4)
*Tweezes (5)
*Perforator (6)
*Glue spatula (7)
*Ruler (8)
*Pencil (9)

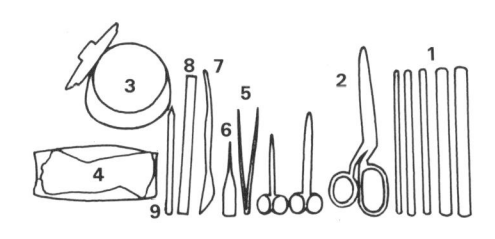

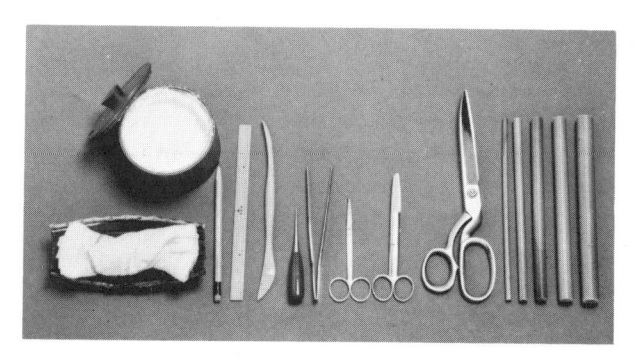

Materials:

Everything from the doll to the miniature items is made of paper when making Japanese paper dolls. It is better not to use ready-made items even for the comb, ornamental hairpins, implements, etc. The following are the main materials. They will vary everytime, depending on what you make.

*Japanese *Shimotsuke* gathered paper
  Use the *Shimotsuke* gathered paper as the Japanese paper. This is paper for arts and crafts which the author, *Shigeo Suwa*, gathers himself by hand. It has a flexibility not found in paper gathered by machine and is the kind of Japanese paper that is easiest to handle. People who cannot get it can use the one gathered by machine.
*Thin, Japanese white paper
*Cut cotton
*Thin drawing paper
*String made from Japanese paper

BASIC *SHIMOTSUKE* DOLL METHOD

A. Head—Body—*Kimono*—Wig—Ornamental hairpins, comb and miniatures.

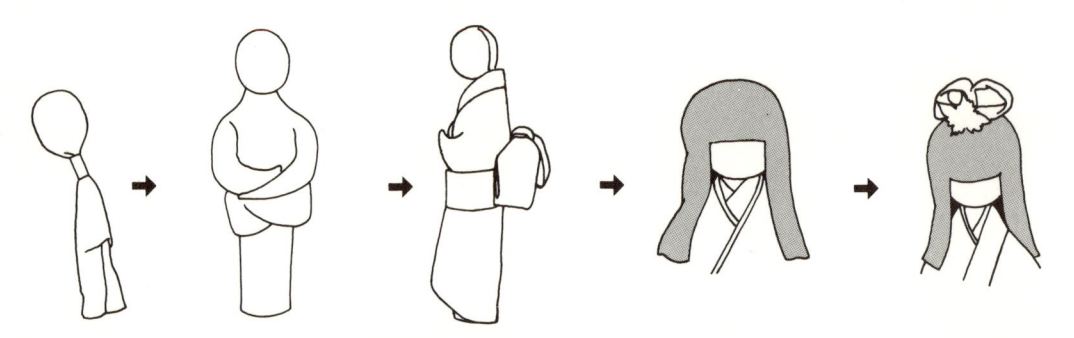

B. Head—Base of the tied up style—Body—*Kimono*—Tied up hair style—Miniatures.

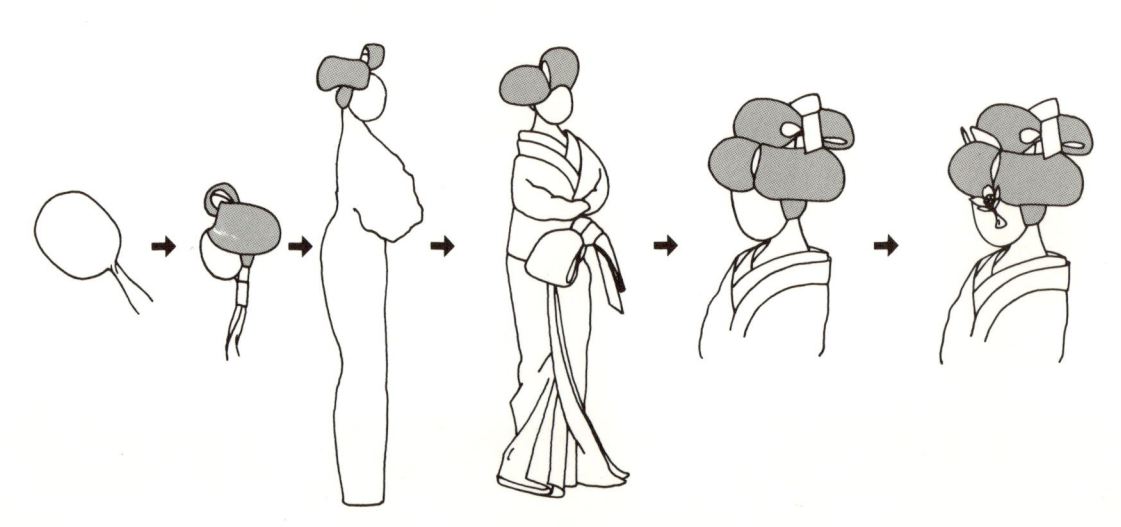

Spring Garden

Hina Dolls

Young *Samurai*

Dwarf

Suihatsu Style

Marumage Chignon

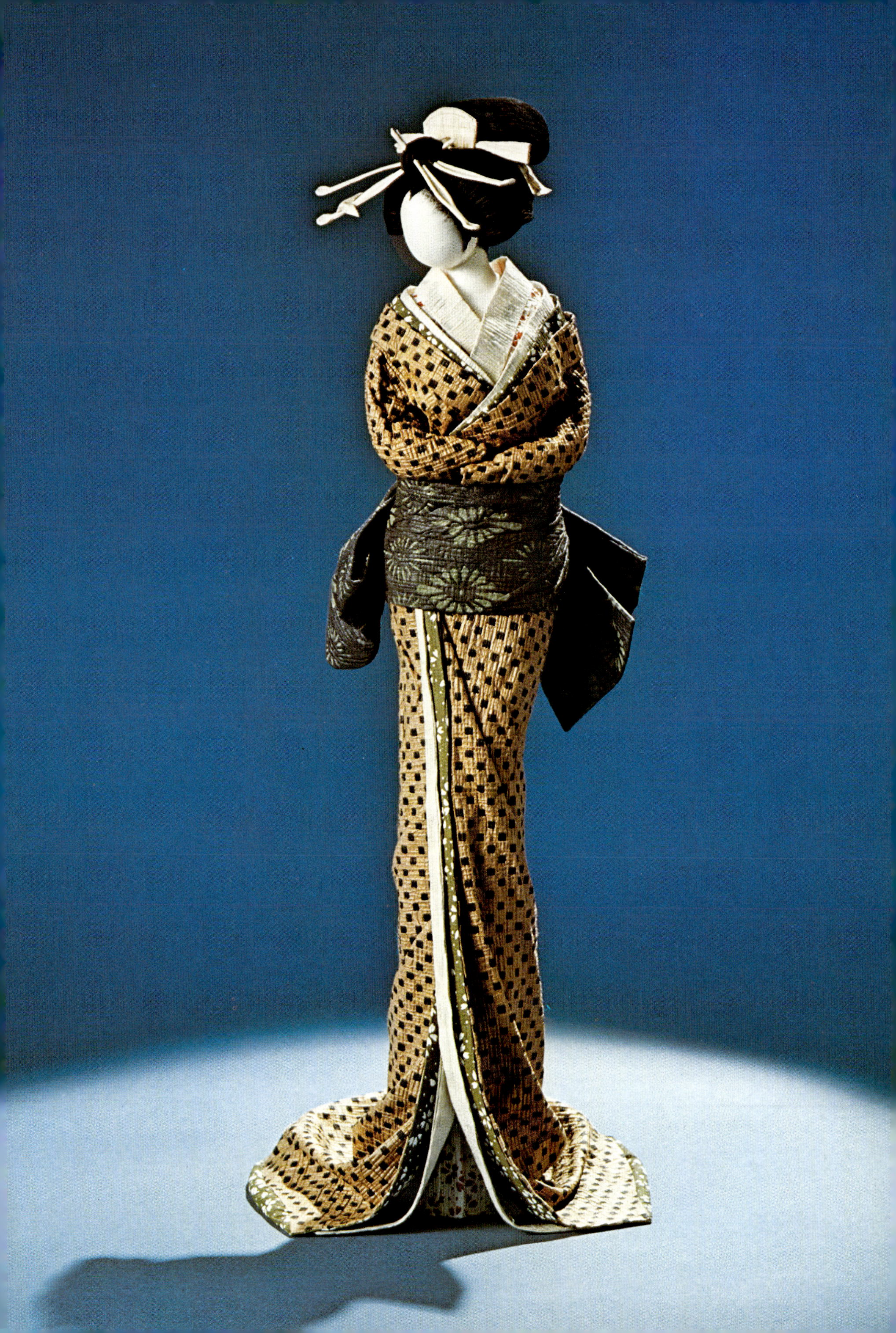

Taka-shimada

Shimada **Chignon**

Momoware **Chignon**

Traveling *Oiran*

15

Tachi-hyogo

BASIC POINT 1
HOW TO MAKE THE HEAD

This is how to make the three basic heads, short bob (child), *samurai's* hair style (three year-old child), and adult (woman). Beginners may well begin with the basic short bob. The body size will be decided in accordance with the size of the finished head. Begin to make it without worrying about the size.

(1) The Basic Short Bob

The short bob is a little girl's hair style. Make this head with the same tender feeling that you have toward your own child.

Materials:
2 pieces of cotton cut to a thickness of 5 mm. (about the size of an ear lobe), plus a little more additional cotton.
2 pieces of thin, white Japanese paper (8.5 × 25 cm.) to be used for the face.
1 piece of thin, white Japanese paper (1 × 5 cm.)

How to Make It
1. Tear 1 piece of the cut cotton down the center with your fingers, dividing it in 2 parts.
2. Divide it again.
3. Roll ⓐ loosely.
4. Put it between both hands and roll it tighter by gently moving your right hand.
5. When you finish rolling it, cut off both ends so that it is the width of your thumb. (If you make it the width of your finger, it will resemble the shape of your own face.)
6. Unroll the end a little, insert ⓑ and roll again. If rolled with the middle finger of the right hand slightly lifted, the chin line will be nicely formed.

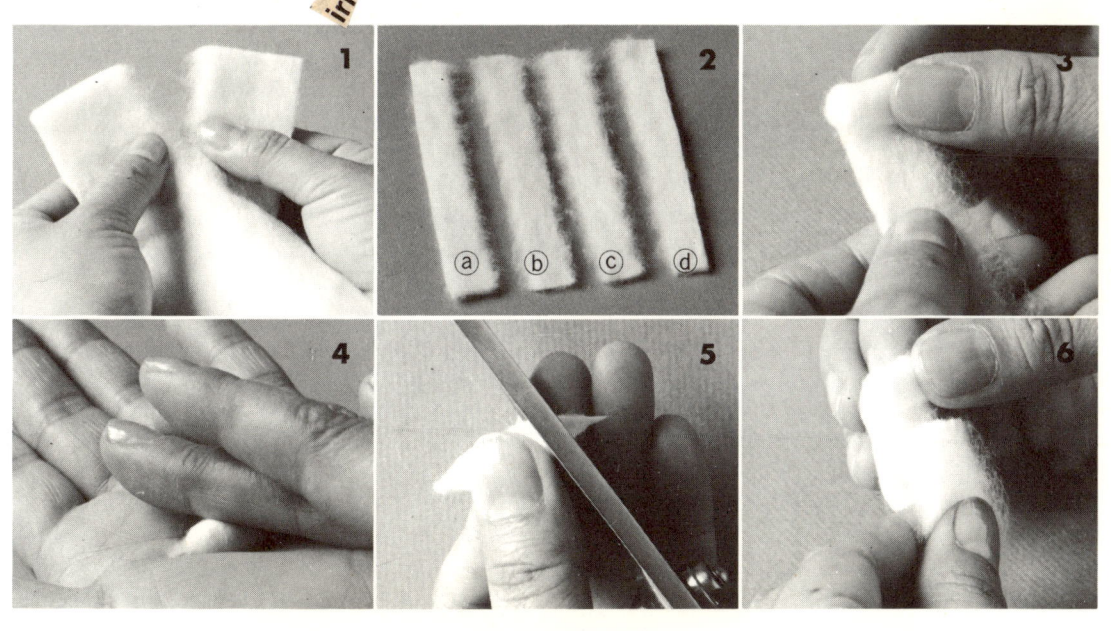

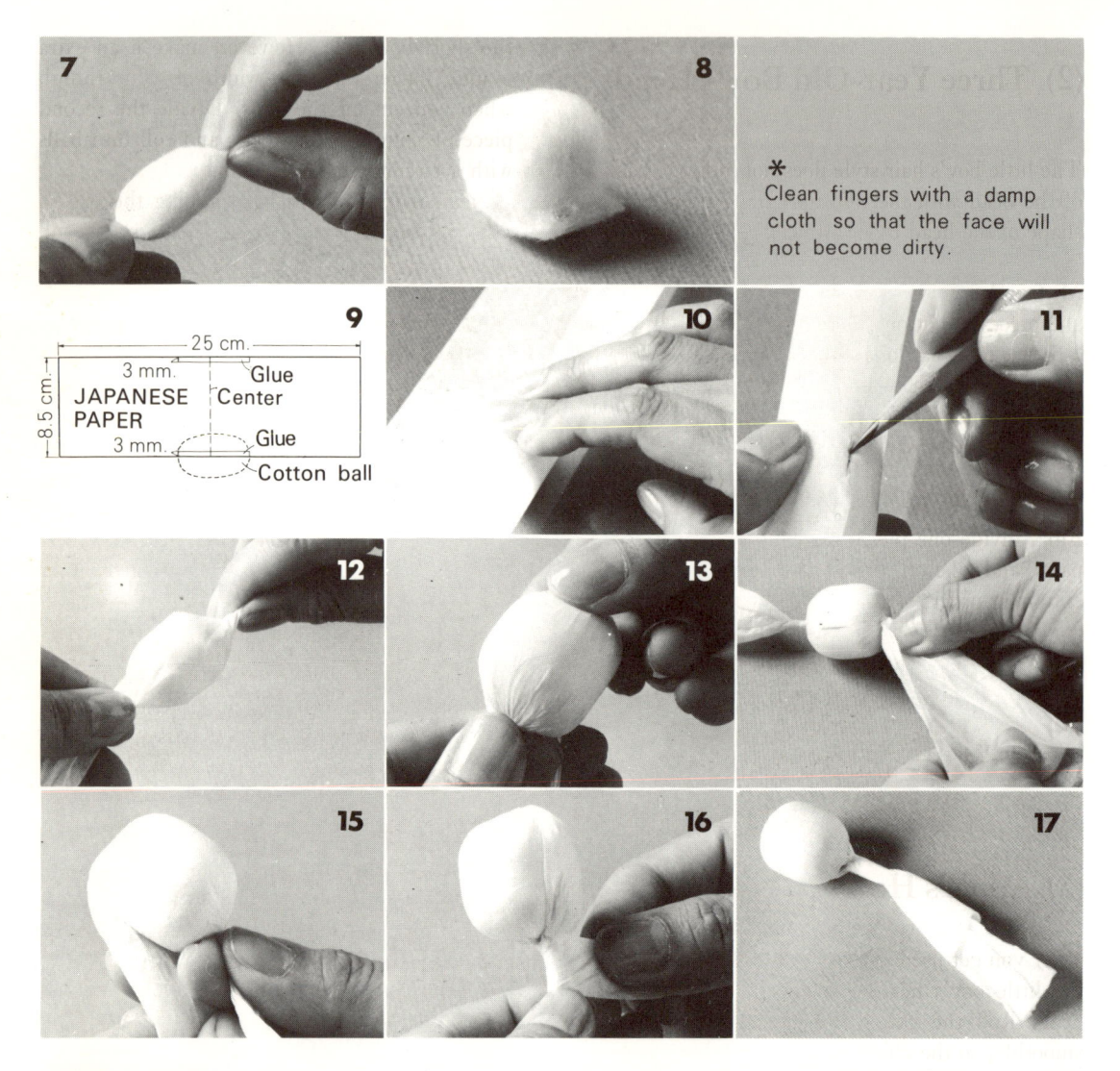

* Clean fingers with a damp cloth so that the face will not become dirty.

7. Twist both ends in oposite directions and cut off the ends.
8. Roll the remaining strips ⓒ, ⓓ likewise. (Take off the edges of the second piece of cut cotton, divide into 3 parts and roll. When rolled 7 times it will have a circumference of 8 cm.) Glue the end of the roll.
9. Next, as shown in the diagram, put glue on the top and bottom of the center of the thin Japanese paper the same width as the cotton ball 3 mm.
10. Place the end of the rolled cotton outside the paper, roll it across and inside.
11. Mark the center of the end of the cotton roll with a pencil. This will be the center of the back of the head.
12. Twist both ends of the head and with the inside of the thumb, smooth out the wrinkles.
13. While taking out the wrinkles, make the cotton ball fit well inside the Japanese paper. It is all right to apply a tiny bit of glue on paper and rub with the fingers.
14. When finished, decide which will be the top and bottom of the face and wrap inside the paper on that side a piece of thin cotton about the same length as your thumb.
15. Next, pull the part with the inserted cotton down over the back of the head and glue.
16. Wrap the 1×5 cm. piece of white Japanese paper around the neck and glue.
17. Now it is finished.

Notice: When making the tied hair style, the head is finished at Step 13, without making the neck.

(2) Three Year-Old Boy's Head

The little boy's hair style does not hide the back of the head with the tied up hair. So make the shape of the head especially neat.

Materials:
- 2 pieces of cotton cut 5 mm. thick (about the size of an ear lobe), plus a little more cotton.
- 1 piece of thin, white Japanese paper for the face (8.5×25 cm.)
- 1 piece of the same paper (1×5 cm.)

How to Make It
First, divide one piece of the cut cotton in five parts, and take off the edges. Roll the strips of cotton in order, starting with, as you did with the short bob style. However, make it an extra 5 mm. longer than the width of your thumb when you cut off the ends. Divide the second piece of cotton in four parts and roll into balls with a circumference of 8 cm.

Next, make the face by wrapping the ball in Japanese paper as you did with the short bob style.

●Tricks of making the back of the head
1. First, spread out the paper on the side that will be the top of the head. Pull it down against the cotton ball and flatten.
2.3. Put a little cotton in under the paper you pulled down and glue. With your finger massage the wrinkles out of the top and back of the head. Do it with glue applied. Then make the neck with the 1×5 cm. piece of paper as you did with the short bob style.

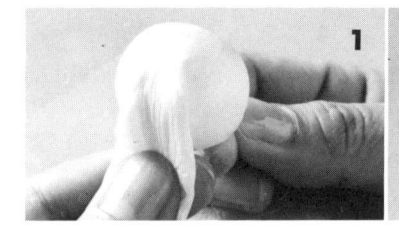

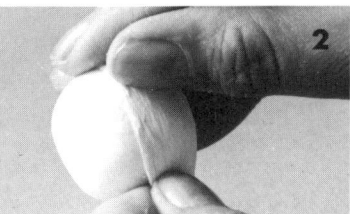

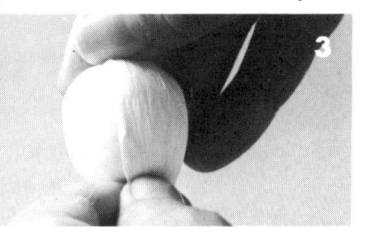

(3) Adult's Head

After you get used to making the short bob and the little boy's heads, try to make the adult's head. Roll the cotton ball inside tightly and smoothly, so the chin line will stand out nicely. The head will be narrower than the children's.

Materials:
- 3 pieces of cotton cut 3 mm. thick.
- 1 piece of thin, white Japanese paper for the face (7.5×25 cm.)

How to Make It
First, divide one piece of cotton in four parts and make the center ball. Divide the second piece in three parts and roll again. It will have a circumference of 7 cm. Put a little glue on both ends. (See the short bob style on p. 17.)

1. Roll the ball in one big piece of cotton you already made.
2. Holding the rolled cotton with both hands, pull both ends with your fingers. It will divide naturally.
3. Twist and close the torn ends.
4. Next, make the center ball fit well. Take off the extra cotton with your fingers, and the chin line will be nice.

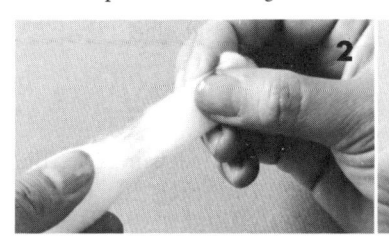

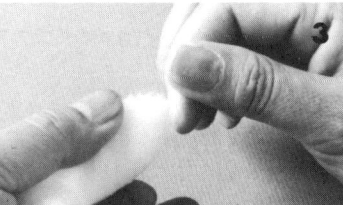

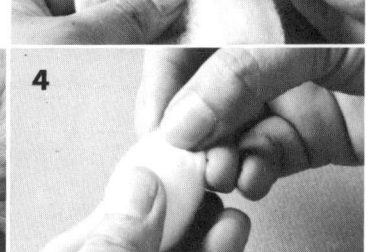

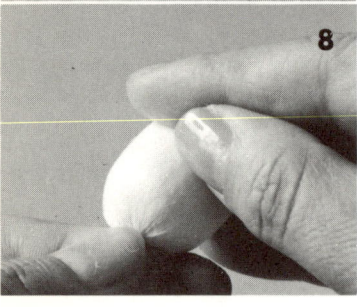

5. Now the cotton ball for the adult's head is finished.
6. Apply glue to Japanese paper and roll the ball inside as you did with the short bob style. Twist both ends. Smooth out the wrinkles in the face with your fingers.
7.8. Neaten the top of the head and chin line. Doing it with glue applied works well.

In the case of the wig hair style, you have to make the neck with tape as was explained in the part on the short bob style (See p. 18). When making the tied up style you make the neck after joining the forelock and the base of the back hair. (See p. 46.)

(4) Various Standard Head Sizes

The basic heads are the previously mentioned short bob style, three year-old boy and adult woman, but there are various others such as the young man, adult man, etc. The next sketch shows the standard head sizes. Use it for reference.

Short bob style head: Make it perfectly round as in the sketch. Make the chin line as a little girl's should look.

Three year-old boy's head: Flatten the top of the head and the bottom of the chin, and it will be even rounder.

Young man's head: The head is about the same length as the short bob style's head, but make the top of the head long and slender and the chin round.

Adult woman's head: The whole head is slender.

Adult man's head: Make the face longer than that of the short bob style's head and the chin line as a man's should be.

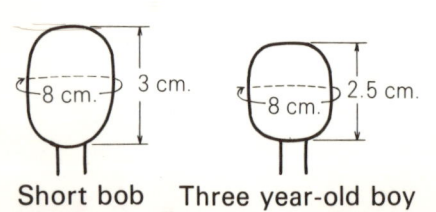

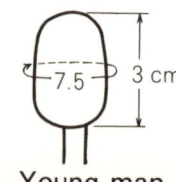

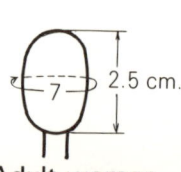

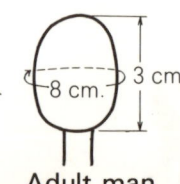

Short bob	Three year-old boy	Young man	Adult woman	Adult man
8 cm. × 3 cm.	8 cm. × 2.5 cm.	7.5 × 3 cm.	7 × 2.5 cm.	8 cm. × 3 cm.

BASIC POINT 2
HOW TO MAKE THE BODY

(1) Child's Body (Basic Model)

Use the basic model for the short bob style head up to where the neck is made. For the tied up style of a little girl, use the head on which the forelock and back hair are joined.

Materials:
- 4 pieces of thin, white Japanese paper for the breast plate (3×12 cm.)
- 4 other pieces of the same paper (1×5 cm.)
- 5 pieces of cotton cut 5 mm. thick for the torso padding.
- 1 piece each of cotton 5 mm. thick and 7 mm. thick for the breast plate.
- 1 piece of drawing paper for the legs.
- String.
- 1 short bob style head.

(a) Torso padding and legs

First, divide the five 5 mm. thick pieces of cotton in two parts, making ten pieces.

1. Place your thumb under the chin and apply glue for about 1 cm. below the thumb, taking care not to loosen the neck.
2. Place the corner of one piece of the cotton 1.5 cm. below the chin diagonally with the long end up. Wind it down and around.
3. Do not force it when winding it down.
4. Put the second piece of cotton at a right angle to the torso.
5. Holding it down between both hands, roll it around tightly.
6. Wind the third piece down and around as you did with the first, starting 5 mm. below the chin.
7. Do the fourth piece as you did the second (4), taking care not to loosen the neck.
8. Wind the fifth piece down and around,

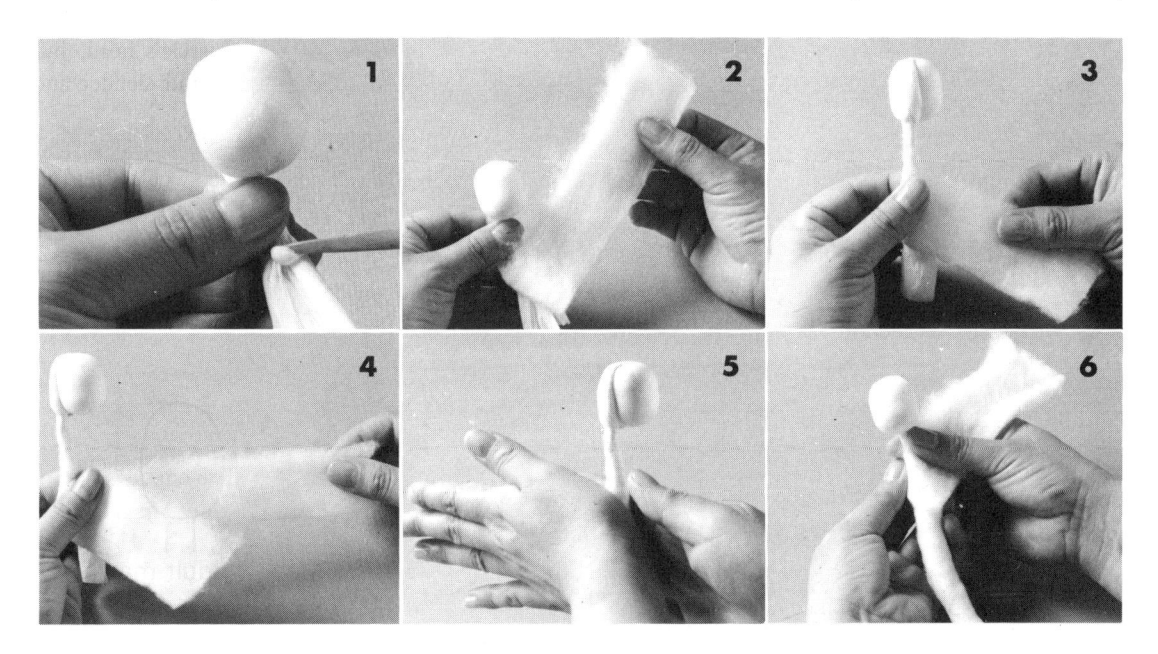

starting right below the chin.
9. Make the base of the neck neat by pulling it with your fingers. Put on the sixth—ninth pieces alternately as you did the first (starting 1.5 cm. below the chin) and second pieces (at a right angle to the torso).
10. Wind the tenth piece around firmly below the hip. When finished, the breast should be about 10 cm. around. From the chin to the bottom should be about 10 cm. in length.
11. Cut the drawing paper 13×18 cm. and apply glue to ¾ of the paper.
12. Place the back of the body in the center of the paper where glue has been applied.
13. Next, wrap the paper firmly around the hips. This will be the legs.
14. Before the glue dries, place your finger where the back of the knees will be and make a dent.
15. Make the cotton inside fit well in the legs and adjust the shape. Now you have put legs on the body.

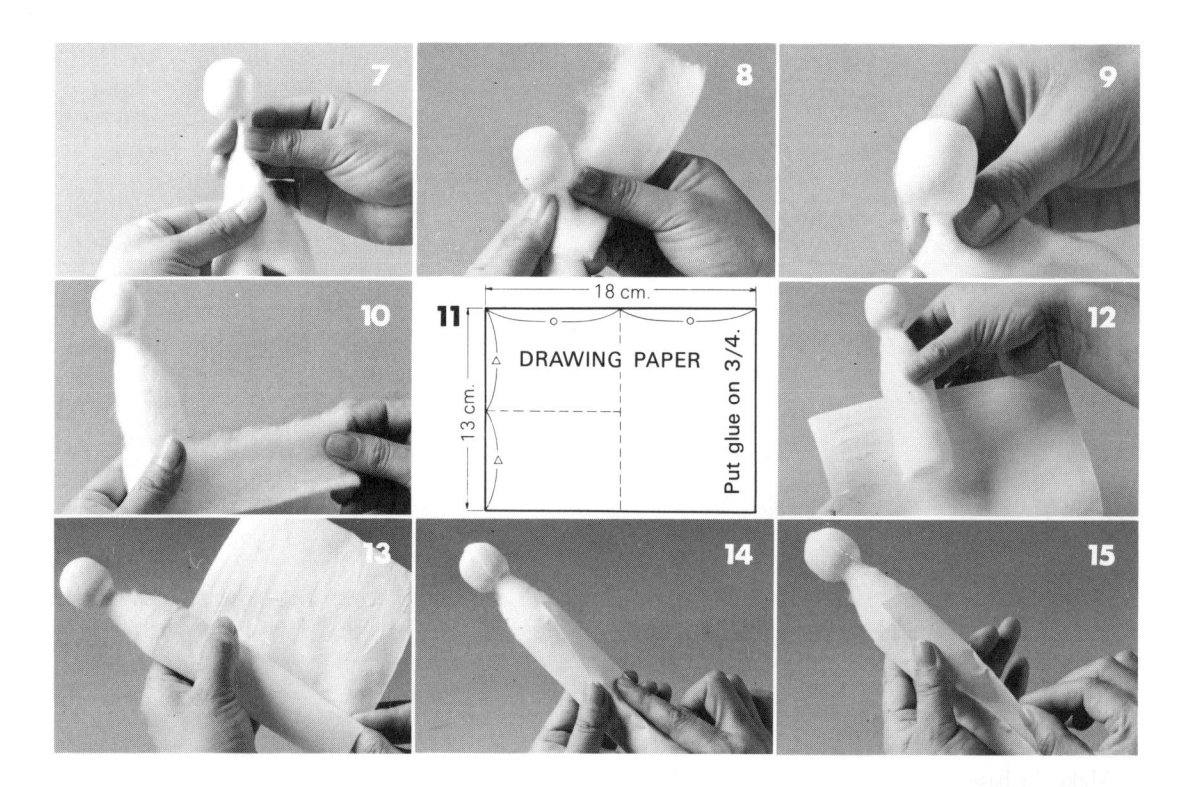

(b) Breast

1. Take the edges off one side of the two pieces of cotton (5 mm. and 7 mm. thick).
2. Place the 5 mm. thick piece against the back and bring it down across the shoulders and down the front of the body.
3. Next, do the same with the 7 mm. thick piece, but from front to back.

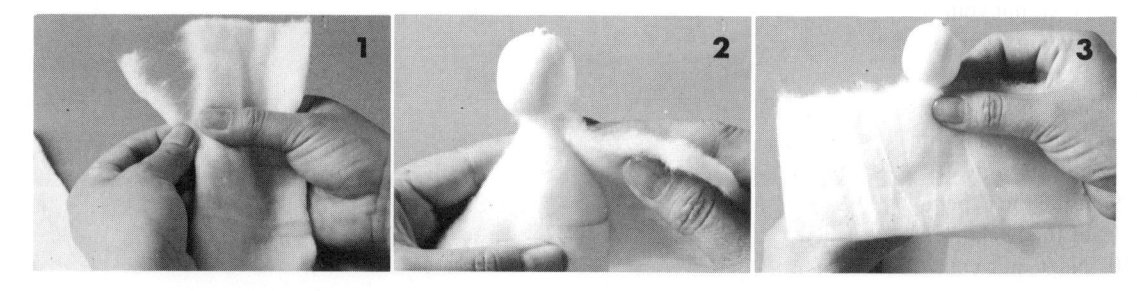

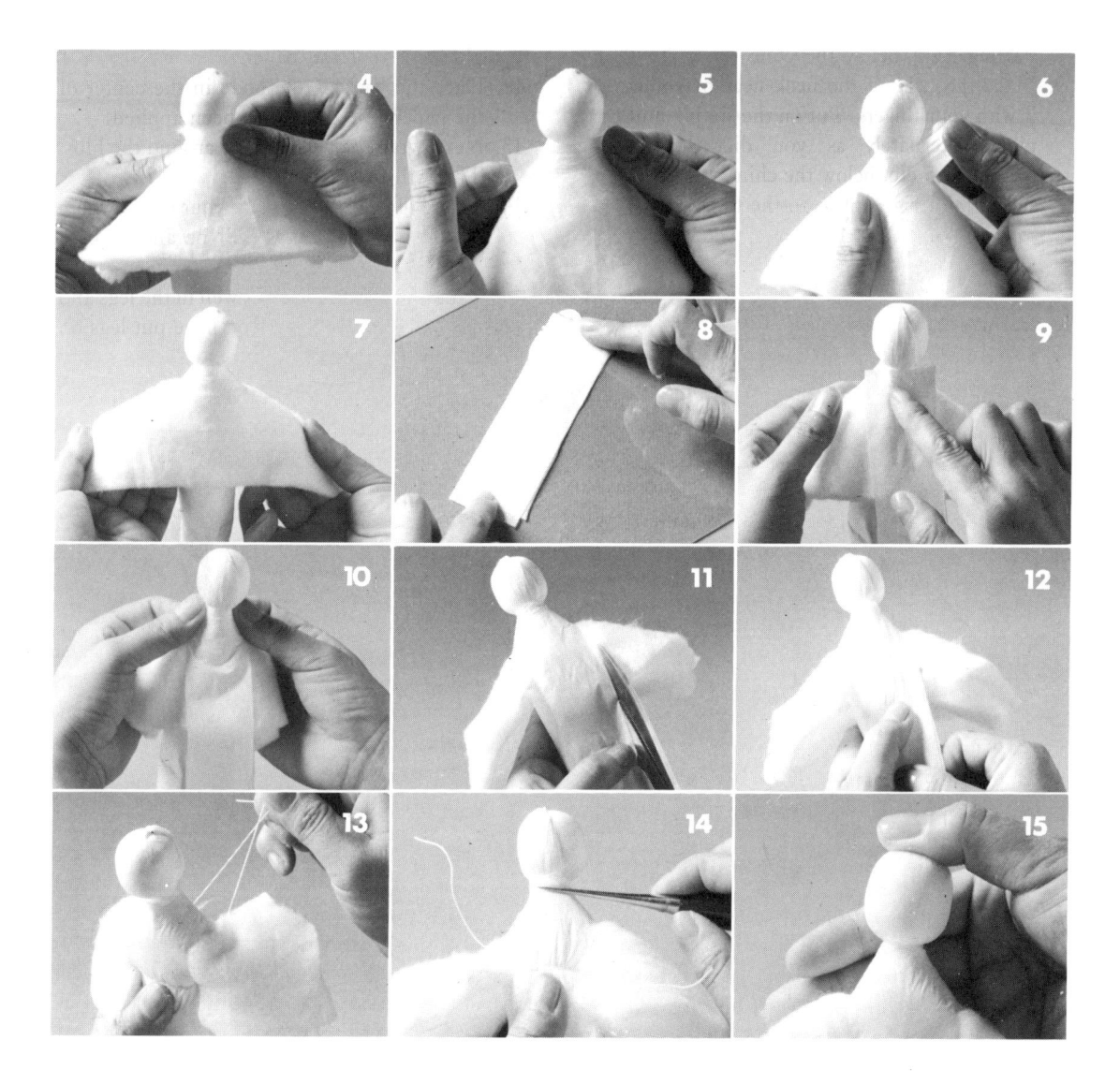

4. Make the base of the neck fit well in the body when putting the cotton pieces on.
5. Put glue on two pieces of paper tape and use them to hold down the front and back of the neck base. Do the back area first.
6. Likewise, glue strips of tape on both shoulders.
7. Next, put your fingers in under the shoulders and adjust the shape.
8. Put two pieces of paper for the breast plate one on top of the other with the side of one about 5 mm. lower than the other. Apply glue to only ⅓ of the paper.
9. Glue the paper gently at the base of the back of the neck in the center only.
10. Next, put your fingers under the shoulders, bring the paper forward around the shoulders and glue. Do likewise with the two remaining pieces of paper from front to back.
11. After gluing on the paper, make 3 cm. long cuts along the body line in both front and back. This will make the sleeves.
12. Straighten the nape of the neck and pull the back paper. Do likewise with the front.
13. Next, put string around the breast from front to back and tie in back.
14. Put glue on the tip of a perforator and make the nape of the neck stationary. Take off extra glue with your finger tip.
15. Give the neck its posture before the glue dries. When the head faces the front, push it forward and down gently.

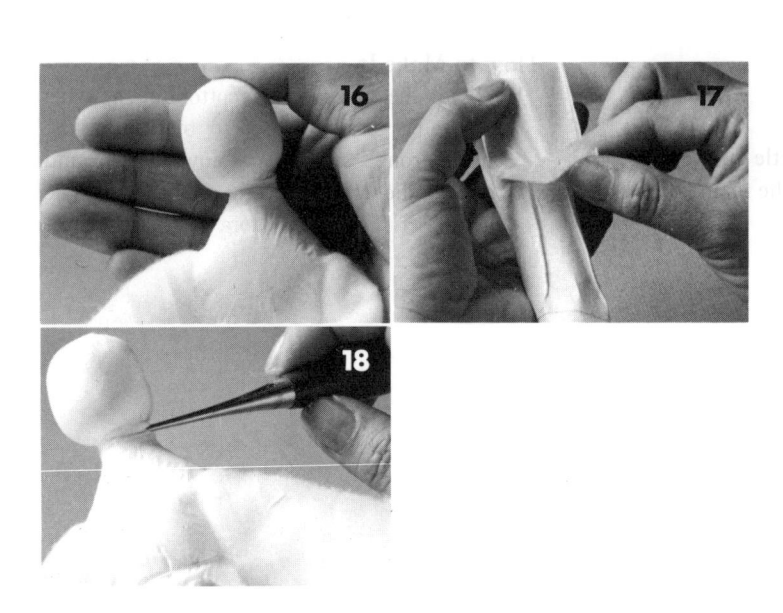

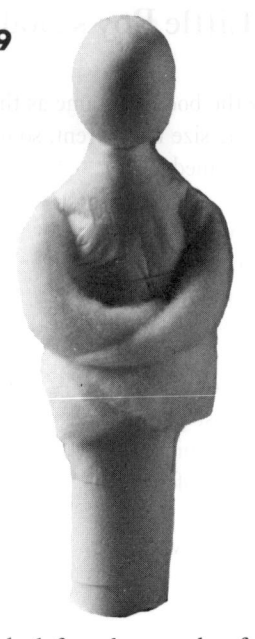

16. When the head tilts to one side or the other, push it down over the shoulders.
17. Glue the front and back hemline of the breast plate.
18. Take out the wrinkles at the neck with a perforator and make the neck neat with your finger tip.
19. The arms may be left as they are, but for the short bob style, overlap the arms in front, left over right and tie with string. The string will be taken out when dressing.

● Tips for beginners
When making dolls for the first time your hands will be unaccustomed. It will be unstable in many ways. If the legs are made using a stand, it will be easier to make them without shaking. Also use a stand when dressing the doll and giving it the finishing touches.

1. Put a wooden tube on a doll stand (on the market anywhere) with nails.
2. Put the torso with cotton wound around it on over the wooden tube. Wrap around the drawing paper with glue applied and glue it.
3. Make tucks below the knees. Steady it and adjust the legs.

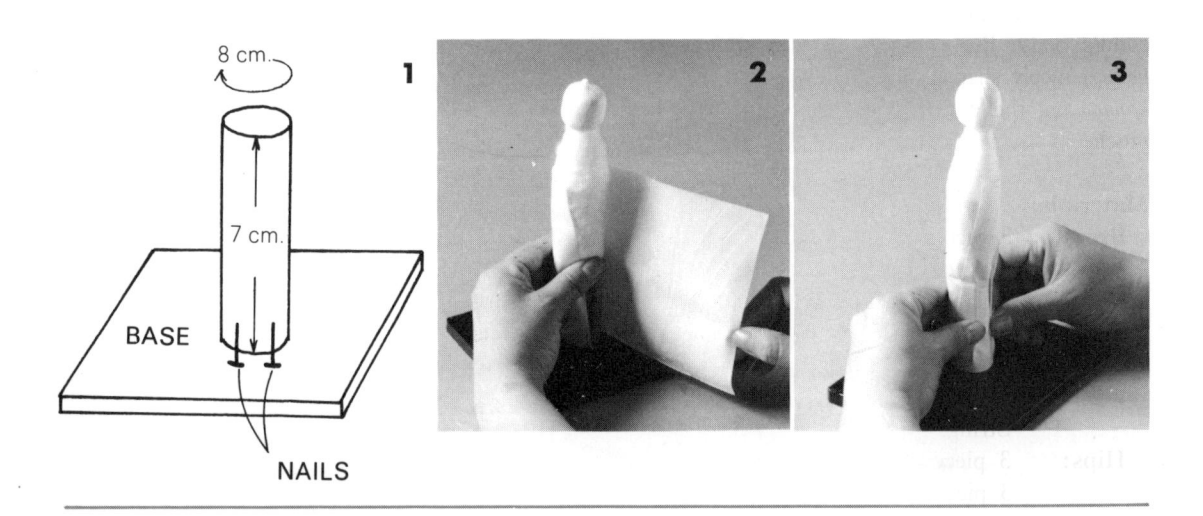

24

(2) Little Boy's Body

Make the body the same as the little girl's body. Only the size is different, so just the main points are explained.

Materials:
- 4 pieces of cotton cut 5 mm. thick for the torso padding.
- 1 piece of cotton 7 mm. thick for the breast plate.
- 4 pieces of thin, white Japanese paper for the breast plate (3×12 cm.)
- 4 other pieces of the same (1×5 cm.)
- 1 piece of drawing paper for the legs.
- String.
- 1 little boy's head.

How to Make It
1. Divide the four pieces of cotton for the torso in two parts. Make the torso by winding the first through sixth pieces down and around as you did with the little girl's body. (The length from chin to bottom should be 7 cm.) Wind the seventh piece on at a right angle and fasten with glue. To make the length from the chin 7 cm., wind the cotton pieces closer together than you did with the little girl's body. (See sketch ①.)
2. Cut the drawing paper as shown in sketch ②. and apply glue to only ³/₄ of it. Wrap around the torso. Make the base as shown in sketch ③. When finished, the length from under the chin to the bottom will be 10 cm.
3. Divide the cotton for the breastplate in two parts. Place around the back and front of the breast with the torn edges up. Glue up the breastplate paper as you did with the child's body.

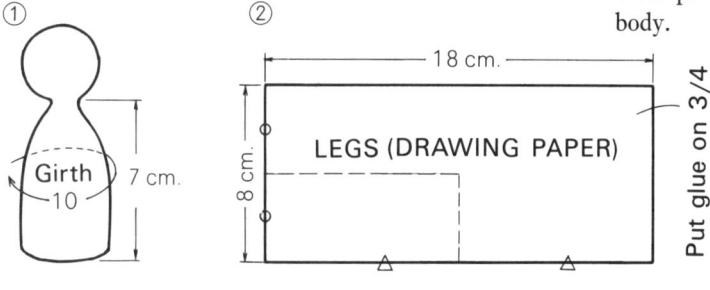

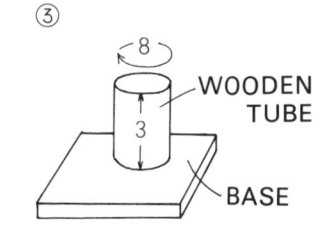

---

(3) Adult's Body

After making the torso, put layer after layer of cotton around the center as you did with the child's body. Put on lots of cotton until you have a nicely shaped body. When you put the *kimono* on, the cotton will not stand out very much.

Materials:
- **Breast:** 3 pieces of cotton cut 7 mm. thick.
  4 pieces of thin, white Japanese paper for the breastplate (3×12 cm.)
  4 other pieces of the same (1×5 cm.)
  String.
- **Hips:** 3 pieces of cotton cut 8 mm. thick.
  3 pieces of thin, white Japanese paper for the bustle (4×25 cm.)
  3 pieces of the same (5×25 cm.)
  String.
- **Calves:** 3 pieces of cotton cut 3 mm. thick.
  4 pieces of white Japanese paper (4×25 cm.)
- **Torso:** 5 pieces of cotton cut 5 mm. thick.
  1 piece of drawing paper for the legs.

How to Make It
First, wind cotton around to make the torso. Make the legs with drawing paper as you did with the child's body. The size will be as shown in the sketch. Cut the drawing paper 18×17 cm. and wrap it around.

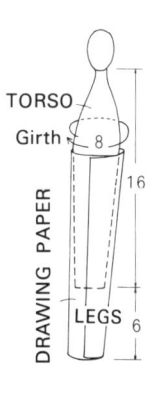

(a) Breast

1. First, get the necessary materials ready. Divide one of the three pieces of cotton (7 mm. thick) in four parts. Take off the edges of the rest.
2. Take two of the four pieces and put one on top of the other, overlapping them only half way.
3. Do likewise with the other two pieces. Put the two groups together one on top of the other with the top edge of the first group 5 mm. lower than that of the second group.
4. Turn over and place the top edge under the chin and put it on the breast of the torso.
5. Put one piece of cotton from back to front and overlap in front.
6. Make the remaining piece of cotton round so that it will bulge.
7. Next, raise the four pieces of cotton piled on the breast with your finger. Fold it toward the torso center and make a bulge.
8. Place the rounded piece of cotton from front to back. Bring it around to the back and form a triangle.
9. Adjust the shape without loosening the neck. Hold the cotton down by gluing on strips of paper tape on the back and front of the neck and one strip on each shoulder.
10. Glue the 3×12 cm. Japanese paper on the front and back of the body as you did with the child's body. (See p. 23.) Next, make cuts in the cotton along the body line to make the sleeves. Tie string tightly around the pit of the stomach.

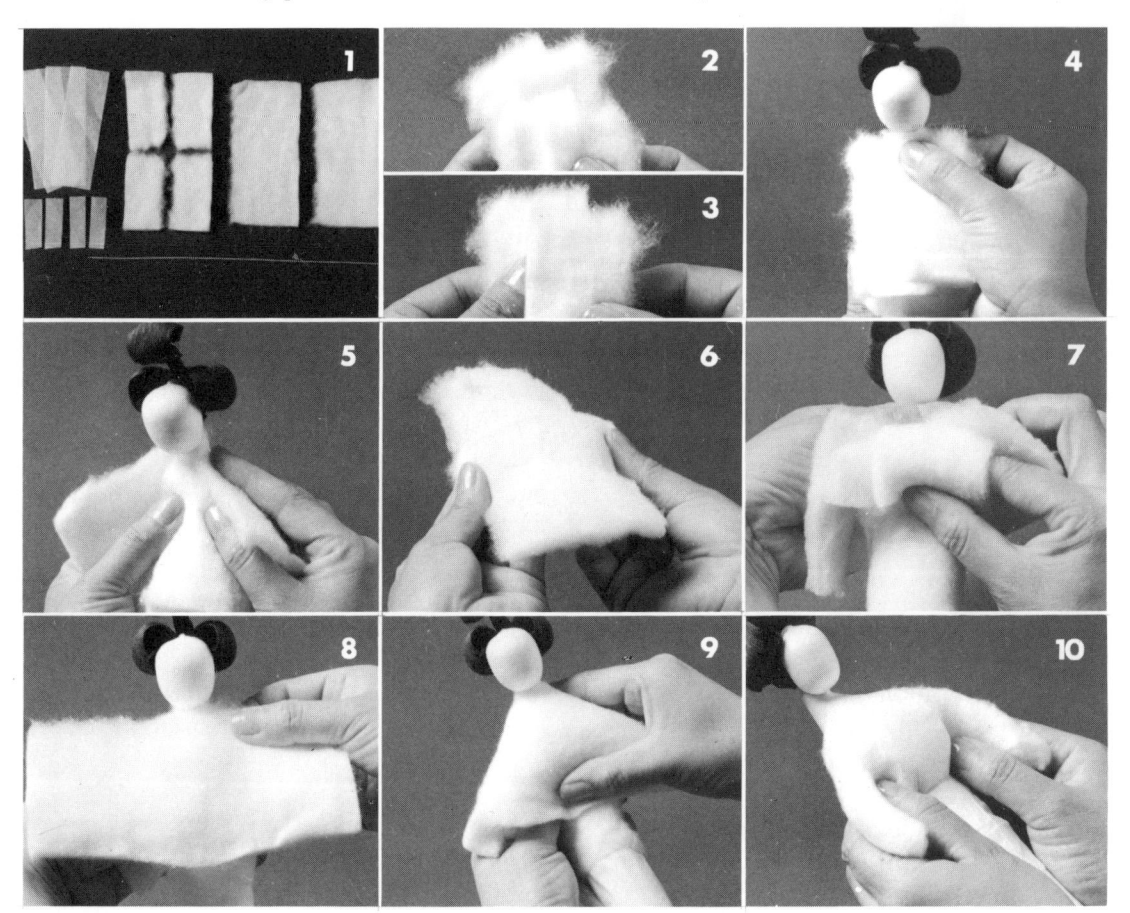

(b) Hips

1. First get the necessary materials ready. Make three groups of Japanese paper with one 4 cm. wide piece on top of one 5 cm. wide piece. Tear the cotton into three oblong pieces. Tear one oblong piece in two parts and another in four parts.
2. Stretch the center of the big oblong piece, making it round so that it will easily be placed against the body.
3. Put the group of two pieces of cotton and the group of four pieces one on top of the other in order.
4. With the smallest pieces on the bottom, place it against the hips in the back. Make it curve naturally.
5. Once you have decided the position of the hips, take the cotton away and put glue in that place on the torso. Looking at the hips from the side, it should form an S in proportion to the breast.
6. Put on the cotton and adjust the shape.
7. Apply glue to each of the three groups of paper, leaving 3 cm. free at each end.
8. Place the first piece on the hip, pull it up diagonally and glue, holding the unglued edges.
9. Tear off the leftover paper in front.

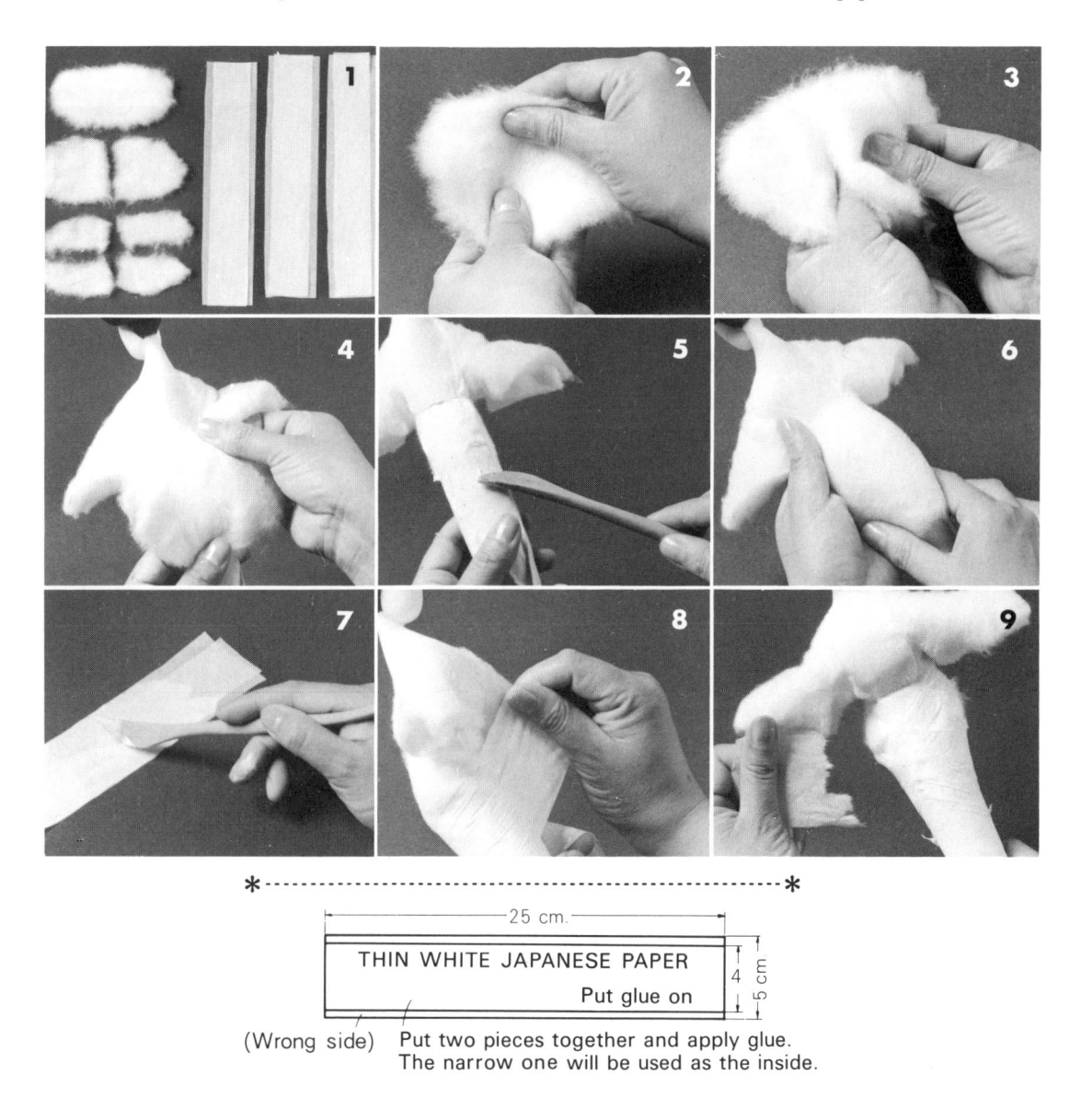

--

```
|-------25 cm.-------|
| THIN WHITE JAPANESE PAPER |  ↑
|                           |  4 cm
|        Put glue on        |  ↓  5 cm
```

(Wrong side) Put two pieces together and apply glue.
The narrow one will be used as the inside.

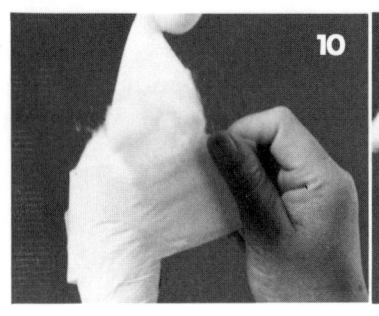

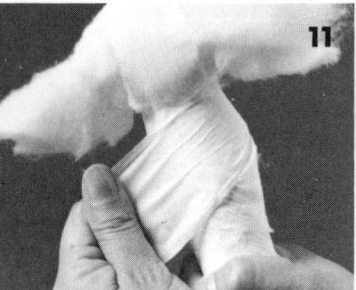

10. Do likewise with the second piece, placing it a little farther up against the hip when beginning. Tear off the leftover poriton.
11. Do likewise with the third piece, starting a little higher than with the previous two pieces, so that the torso is held down. Tear off the leftover portion.
12. Now the hips are nicely rounded.

(c) Calves

Get the cotton and Japanese paper ready as you did for the hips and make the calves. (See sketch 4–7). Shape the beautiful form of the body with the Japanese paper. How to apply the paper and the order in which to do it is shown in the sketch. Dress the doll after the glue dries. (Photo: under)

(4) Body Model

The proportions of the body will differ according to the head size and the height of the hairdo.

The sketch shows the average proportions, an adult's body eight heads high and a child's body five heads high. The length of the face is standard size. Make the proportions of the young man's body and the little boy's body the same. If you put on a hair style with a topknot, make the legs longer in proportion to it.

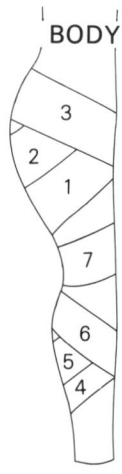

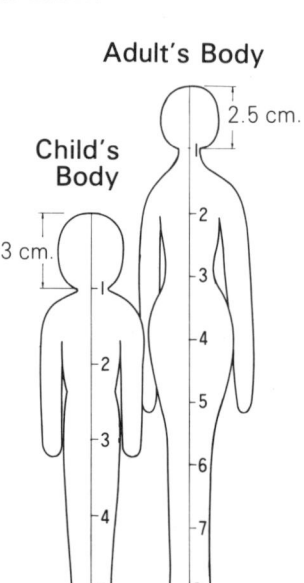

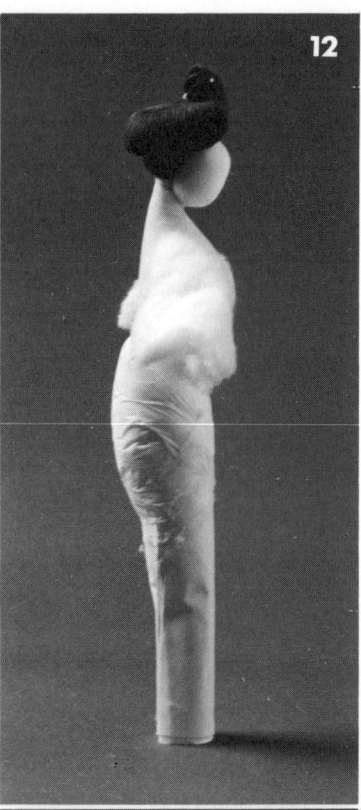

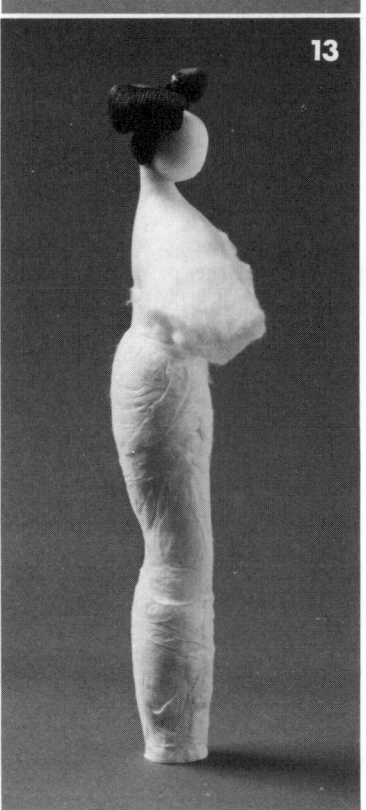

BASIC POINT 3
KIMONO

(1) Child's *Kimono*

It is easy to put on *kimono* if you make it into a two part, with a tuck at the waist. You may fold in a tuck at the waist and not make two parts. Choose a design, *obi*, etc. which harmonize well.

Materials:
1 piece of gathered paper with a print for the *kimono* (20×26.5 cm.)
1 piece of solid color gathered paper for the lining (20×26.5 cm.)
1 piece of solid color gathered paper for the neckband (3.5×11 cm.)
1 piece of gathered paper with a print for the *obi* (7×42 cm.)
1 piece of drawing paper for the lining.
1 pattern for a child's *kimono* (See the sketch.)
1 child's body.

(a) *Kimono*

First, place the pattern on the paper for the *kimono* and the lining and decide the position of the collar, cuffs and hemline. Leave a place to put glue (3 cm. at the collar, 1 cm. at the cuffs, 1.5 cm. at the hemline).

1. Place the pattern in the decided position on the wrong side of the paper for the *kimono*. Make 3 cm. cuts under the sleeve bottom. Fold the excess paper at the edge over the pattern at the hemline, lapel, collar, in that order.
2. Next, place the paper for the *kimono* with the pattern still inside on the wrong side of the lining paper. Make 3 mm. cuts under the sleeve. Fold the excess paper over the lapel and hemline, in that order.
3. Take out the pattern and insert the hemline of the lining in the *kimono*.
4. After inserting it, put a little glue 3 mm. from the edge of the bottom corners of the *kimono*. Do likewise on the lapel and hemline. Glue the lining and *kimono* together. This is the *hirazuma* style, so the skirt of the lining is turned out and glued.
5. Put the pattern at a place 8 mm. from the fold of the *kimono* collar and fold back the

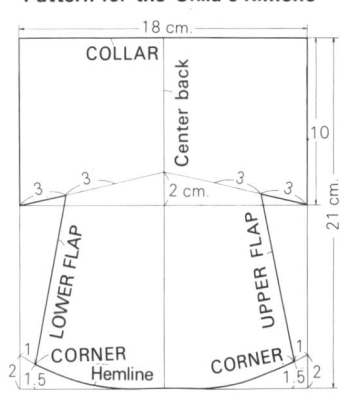

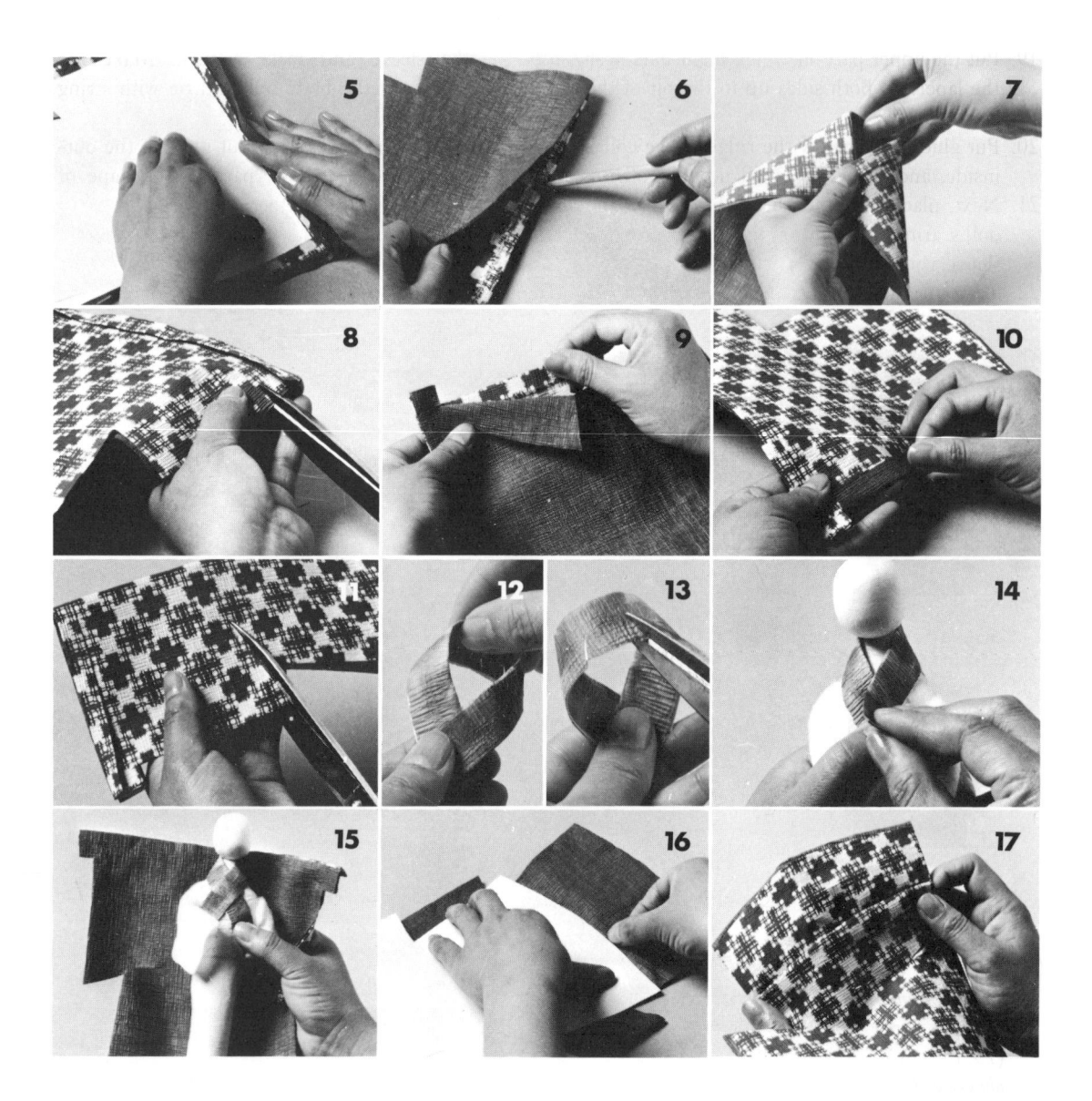

kimono and lining.

6. Put glue on the turned-in edge of the *kimono*. Using the fold just made in the lining, fold the edge of the lining in again and glue.
7. Next, bend the collar, so it will fit easily when put on.
8. Make a 1 cm. long cut 1.5 cm. from the collar and parallel to it.
9. Fold 1 cm. of the cuff edge in from the place where you made the cuts.
10. Fold the lining along the fold of the *kimono*. With this as the fold, turn it inside and glue to the *kimono* edge. The edge of the lining will stick out a little.
11. Fold the *kimono* exactly in half, making the center back seam. Make 3 cm. cuts under the sleeves.
12. Next, line the neckband with drawing paper. Fold in half from end to end and round it, so it will fit the neck.
13. Make 8 cm. cuts in the shape of ⌒ in the center back of the neckband.
14. Place the neckband around the neck and glue.
15. Next, try the *kimono* on. The extra (about 3 cm.) will be the tuck at the waist.
16. Put the hemline of the pattern 3 cm. below the sleeve bottom and make a mark with your fingernail.
17. Fold the tuck at the waist.
18. With the waist tuck as it is, curve it from the sleeve bottom. Cut in two parts.

19. Put the upper part on. Then make cuts near the lapels on both sides up to the pit of the stomach.
20. Put glue 1 cm. below the ridge of the collar inside, and the *kimono* will not slip off.
21. Next, place your thumb on the joint of the doll's arm and adjust the shape of the sleeve with your left finger.
22. Take an adequate amount of the width of the sleeve and make a tuck. Make the *kimono* fit the body well and tie with string temporarily.
23. Put on the lower part. Put glue on the outside flap of the lower part in the shape of $>$ and bring together.
24. Next, put your thumb inside the legs, press in with your other fingers and adjust the shape of the back of the legs.

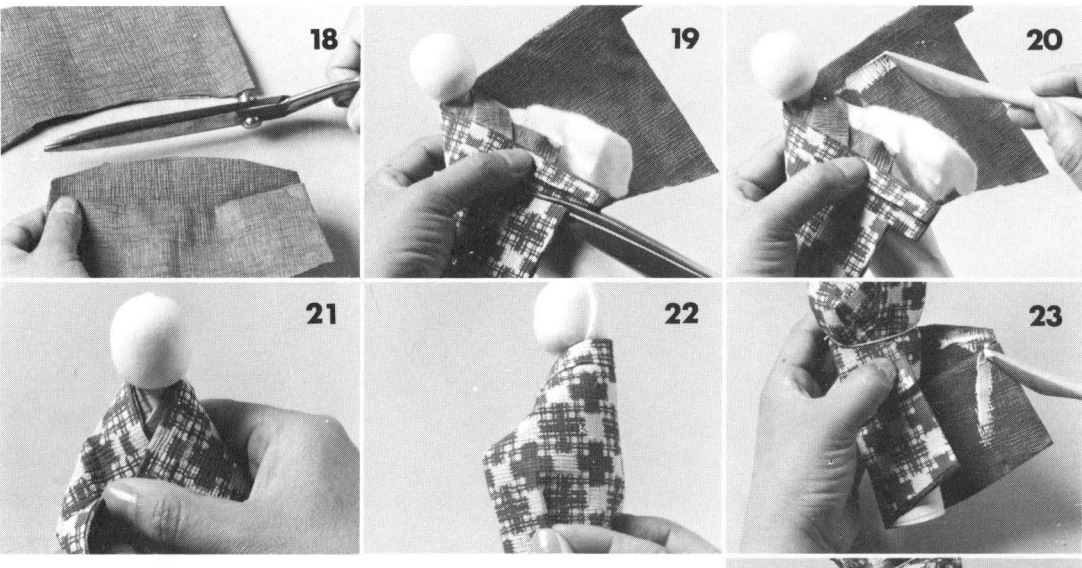

(b) *Obi*

The size of *Bunko Obi* does not have to be exact.
1. Cut the paper for the *obi* into the front *obi* (7×15 cm.), back *obi* (7×20 cm.) and *obi* cover (7 cm. sq.) and line each piece with drawing paper cut the same size. Both ends of the front *obi* will extend 1 cm. longer than the lining.
2. Fold the front *obi* to a width of 2.5 cm. as shown in the sketch.
3. Put the front *obi* on around the body.

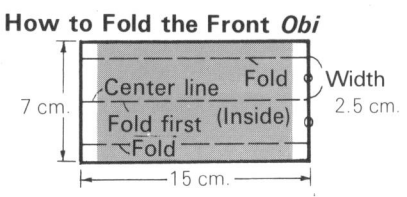

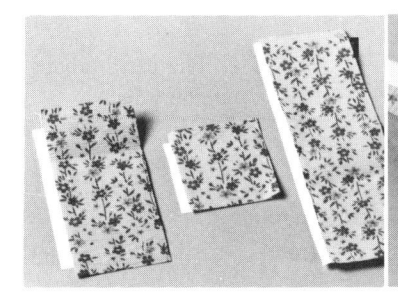

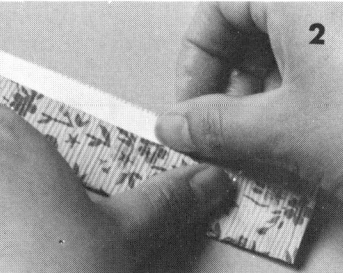

How to Fold the Front *Obi*

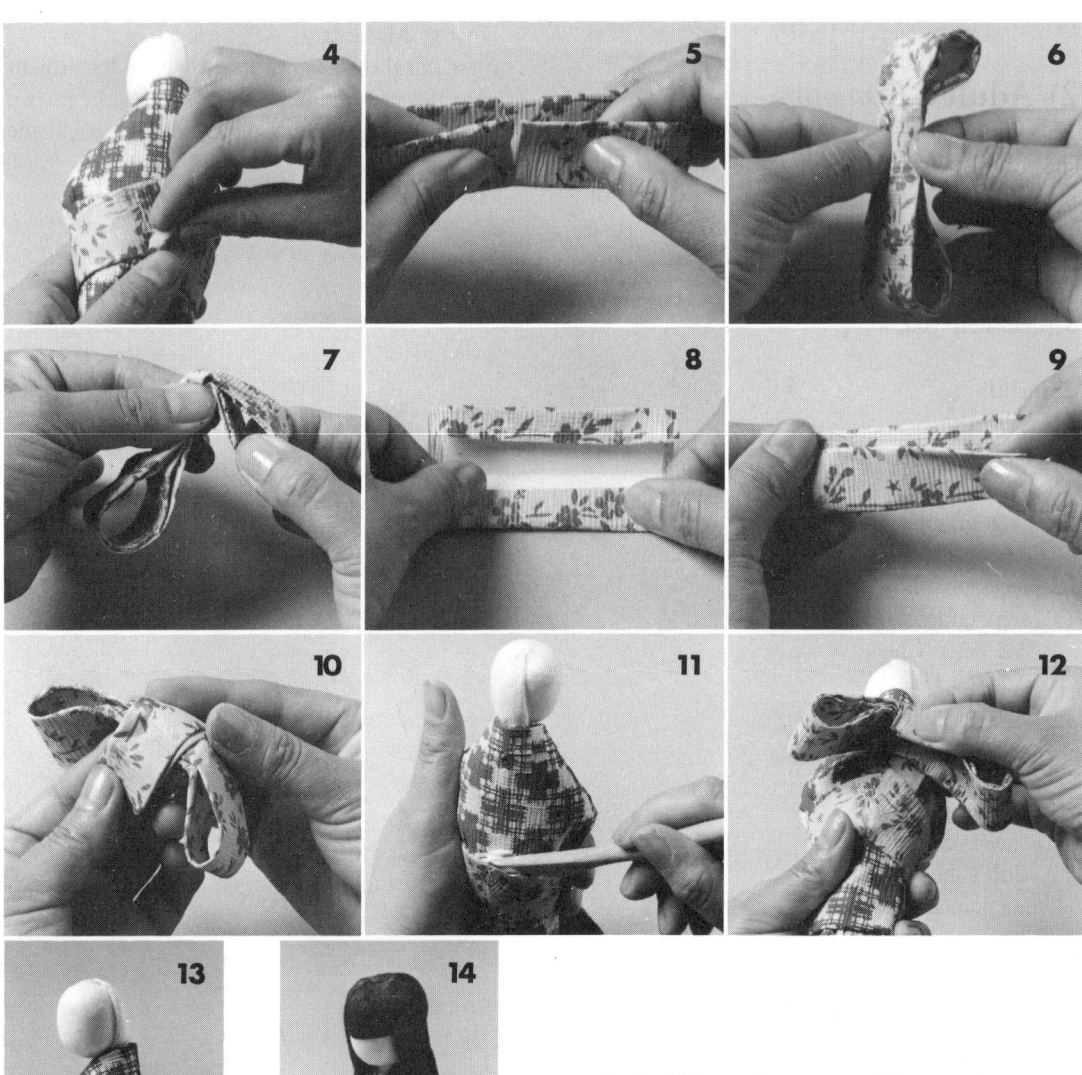

7. Hold it at the center with your fingers and pull both ends to shape the *obi*.
8. Line the *obi* cover. After folding both ends, fold again lengthwise at the center.
9. Fold it so that one edge is slightly below the other.
10. Put the *obi* cover on over the back *obi* and adjust the shape. Make the part to be inserted long.
11. Put glue between the body and the front *obi*.
12. Insert the tab of the *obi* corer and glue. Also secure the other end of the *obi* cover.
13. Make the *obi* fit the body well.
14. Put the short bob hairdo on the head. (See p. 40.) Now the little girl doll is finished. You can make her even cuter by putting on various hair decorations. (See p. 42.)

4. Put glue in the center back of the body, gently fold in the ends and glue.
5. Line the back *obi*. Fold it as you did the front *obi*. Bring the ends together and glue.
6. Pinch a little at the center and make a tuck. This will be the knot.

(2) Adult's *Kimono*

The adult's *kimono* is about the same as the child's, but the space between the collar and neck and the way of putting it together are different. The print of the *kimono*, the degree of overlapping, the *obi*, etc. will differ according to what doll you want to make.

Materials:

(a) *Kimono*

1 piece of gathered paper with a print for the *kimono* (22×31.5 cm.)

1 piece of solid color gathered paper for the lining (22×31.5 cm.)

2 pieces of solid color gathered paper for the long undergarment and its lining (22×31.5 cm.) Choose a color that will go well with the *kimono*.

1 piece of solid color gathered paper for the neckband (3.5×12 cm.)

1 piece of drawing paper of the same size for the lining.

1 *kimono* pattern (See p. 34.)

1 adult's body (with the forelock and back hair joined)

How to Make It

First, cut the *kimono* and the long undergarment after the pattern. Glue together and cut in two parts as you did with the child's *kimono*. Line the neckband.

1. Make cuts in the lined neckband as shown in the sketch (p. 34) and put it on the body. The neckband should be pulled out about 1.5–2 cm. from the back hair. Do not force it.
2. Put the upper garment on and check the opening at the back of the neck.
3. Fold the part that extends over the neckband over again to make it fit.
4. Put it against the neckband and try it on. After fitting it, put glue on the back of the collar and glue.
5. Hold the joint of the arm down with your finger and shape the sleeve.
6. Overlap the sleeves a little at the end, left over right.
7. Next, put the lower *kimono* and lower undergarment together and glue in the center to secure them.
8. Try on the lower garments and overlap in front.
9. After deciding where they will overlap, hold them firmly behind the knees.

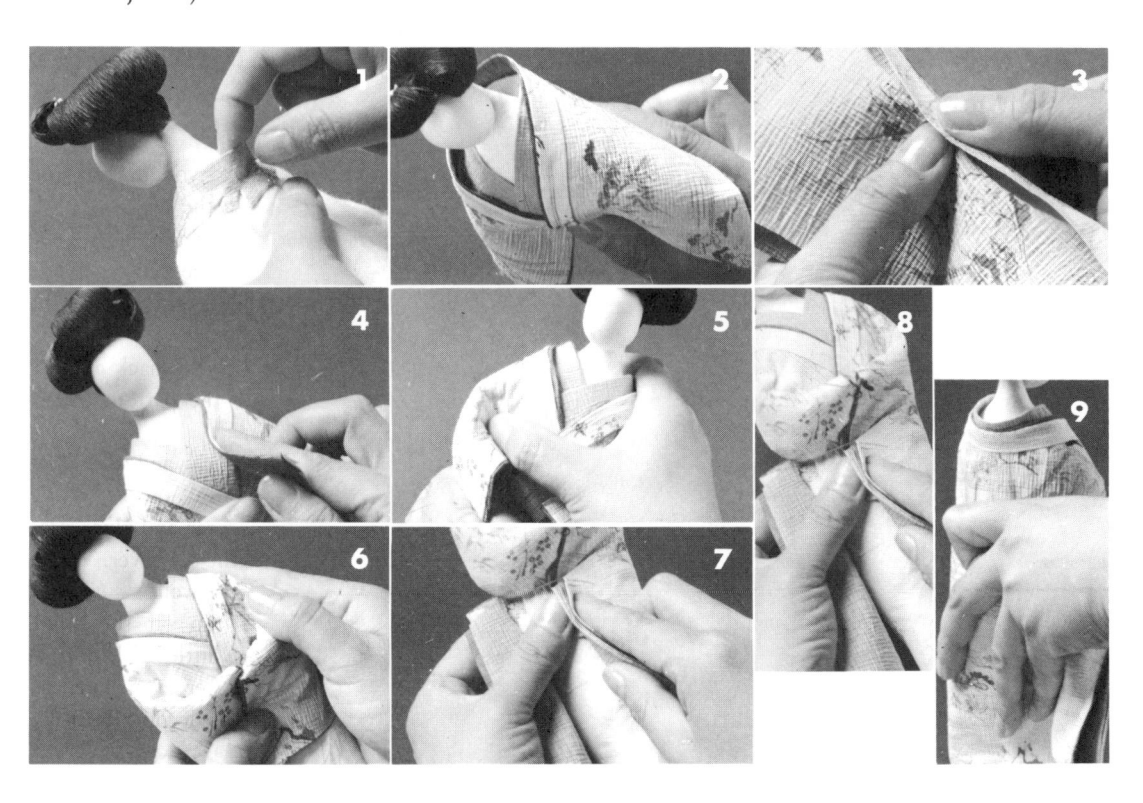

10. Make the bottom corner of the right overlapping part turn out.
11. Overlap in front, left over right, and secure along the top with glue put here and there. Leave the bottom open.

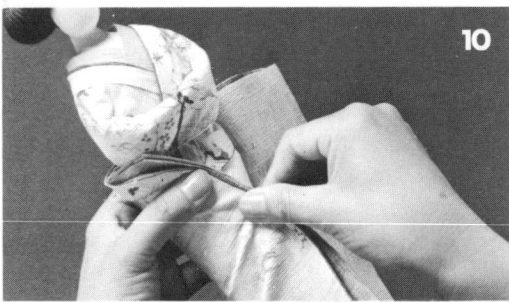

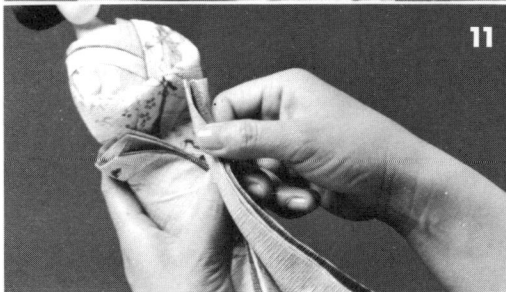

Pattern for the Adult's *Kimono*

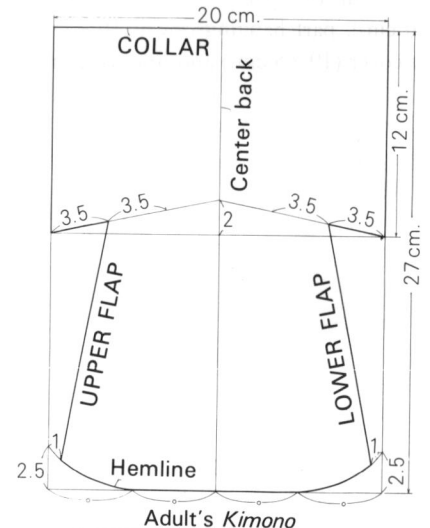

Adult's *Kimono*

To make a train in the back.
To extend the hemline.

● **Variations of the *Kimono* Pattern**
You may want to make the hemline longer or make a train, according to what doll you are making. In that case, make the following pattern. (See the pattern model on the right.)

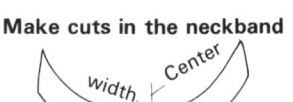

Make cuts in the neckband

(3) Adult's *Obi*

Try many different *obis* on the *kimono* you have made. There are many ways to tie an *obi*. The girth of the waist will differ according to the doll, so adjust the size of the front *obi* accordingly. Choose a becoming color of paper and style of *obi*.

Sageobi (p. 12) ★

This is a narrow *obi* which hangs down. It is put on the *Tachi-Hyogo* Dolls, etc.

Materials:
1 piece of gathered Japanese paper with a print for the *obi* (10×49 cm.)
1 piece of drawing paper for the lining.

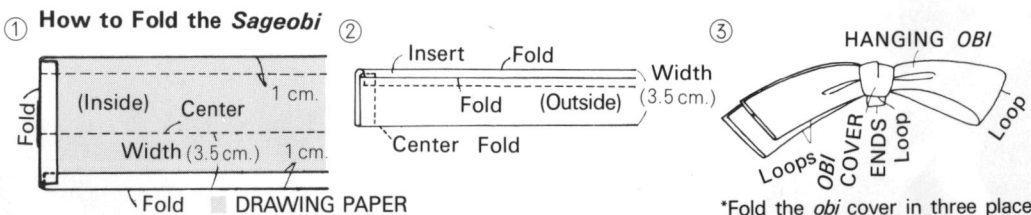

① **How to Fold the *Sageobi***

②

③ **HANGING *OBI***

*Fold the *obi* cover in three places.
*Fold it unevenly all over, make a natural tuck in the center.

34

How to Make It

First, cut out the parts of the *obi*: front *obi* (10×16 cm.), part hanging down (10×25 cm.), and *obi* cover (10×8 cm.) and line with drawing paper.

1. Fold the front *obi* to a width of 3.5 cm. Bring it around from back to front (opposite of the child's *obi*) and glue. Make a small tuck in the front.
2. Cut off any extra at the ends and overlap in front about 5 mm.
3. Make the part that hangs down as shown in the sketch. Insert the tabs in the front *obi*.

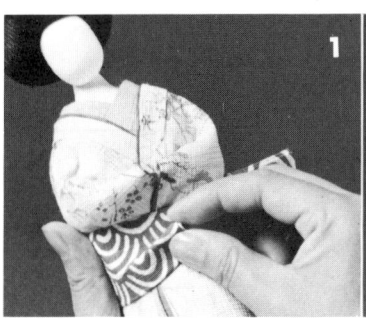

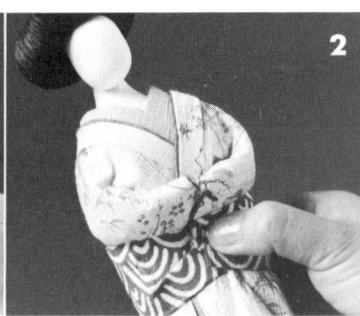

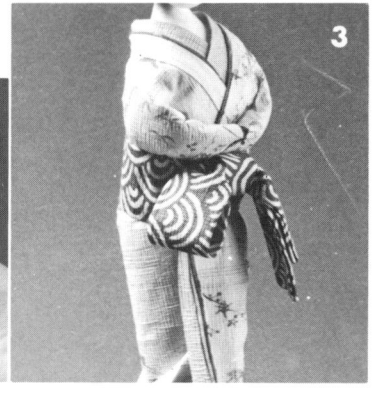

Hosoobi (pp. 9, 16) ★

This is narrower than the *Sageobi* and is tied in the front or back. It is worn with the ponytail or tied up hairdo.

Materials:

1 piece of gathered paper with a print for the *obi* (7×54 cm.)
1 piece of drawing paper for the lining.

How to Make It

First, cut out the parts: front *obi* (7×16 cm.), hanging part (7×30 cm.), *obi* cover (7×8 cm.) and line with drawing paper of the same size.

1. Fold the front *obi*. Wind it around the waist, bring the ends together in back and glue. Cut off the excess ends. Fold the ends and bring them together.
2. Fold the hanging part. (See p. 34.)
3. Fold the hanging part in a nice shape. Make the end that will hang down long. Put the *obi* cover on and adjust.
4. Insert the tabs of the *obi* cover behind the front *obi*.

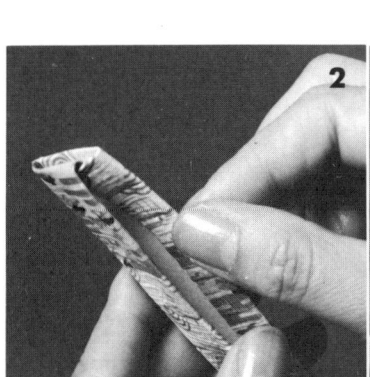

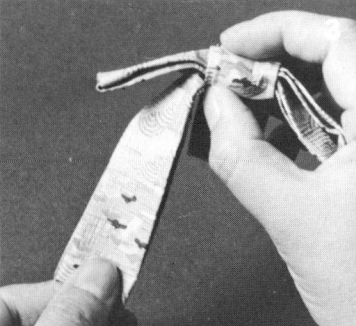

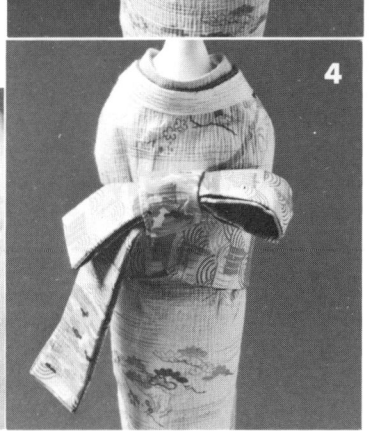

Taiko Obi (p. 14) ★

This is the most popular *obi* style. It looks nice if it is slightly larger. The literal meaning of *taiko* is a "drum."

Materials:
1 piece of gathered paper with a print for the *obi* (18×32 cm.)
1 piece of drawing paper for the lining.

How to Make It
First cut out the *obi* parts: front *obi* (8×32 cm.), drum (10×25 cm.), side flaps (10×21 cm.) and line them with drawing paper of the same size.

1. Fold the front *obi* to a width of 4 cm. Fold the edges over and glue.
2. Wind the *obi* around once, starting from the center front.
3. Make a tuck in the ends in back and glue. If it does not fit well, wrap a padding of cotton in the Japanese paper around the waist and then put on the *obi*.
4. For the drum fold the paper to a width of about 5 cm. (It will be wider than the front *obi*.) Fold both ends inside. (See how to fold the drum, sketch 1.)
5. Fold over three times, making folds ⓐ, ⓑ, ⓒ. (See sketch 2.)
6. Next, make a 3 cm. cut in fold ⓒ.
7. Overlap the sides of the cut and glue.
8. Make fold ⓐ. With the inside facing out, make tucks in the end and fold inside. Join with the part done in Step 7.
9. Adjust the shape.
10. Next, fold the side flaps to a width of 5 cm. and bend so that both ends are joined in back.

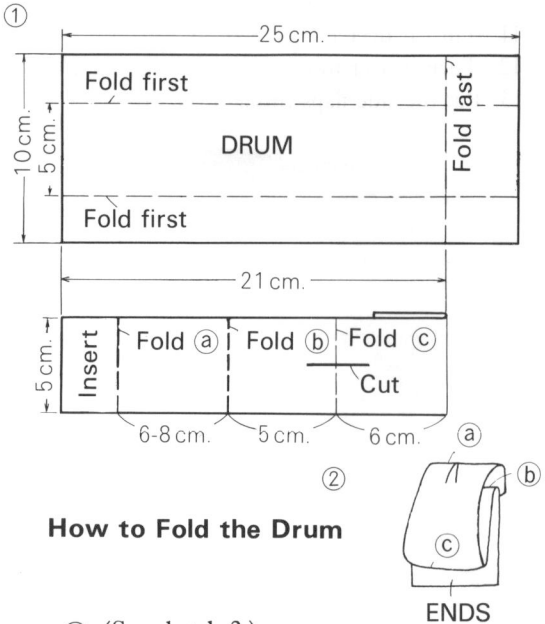

How to Fold the Drum

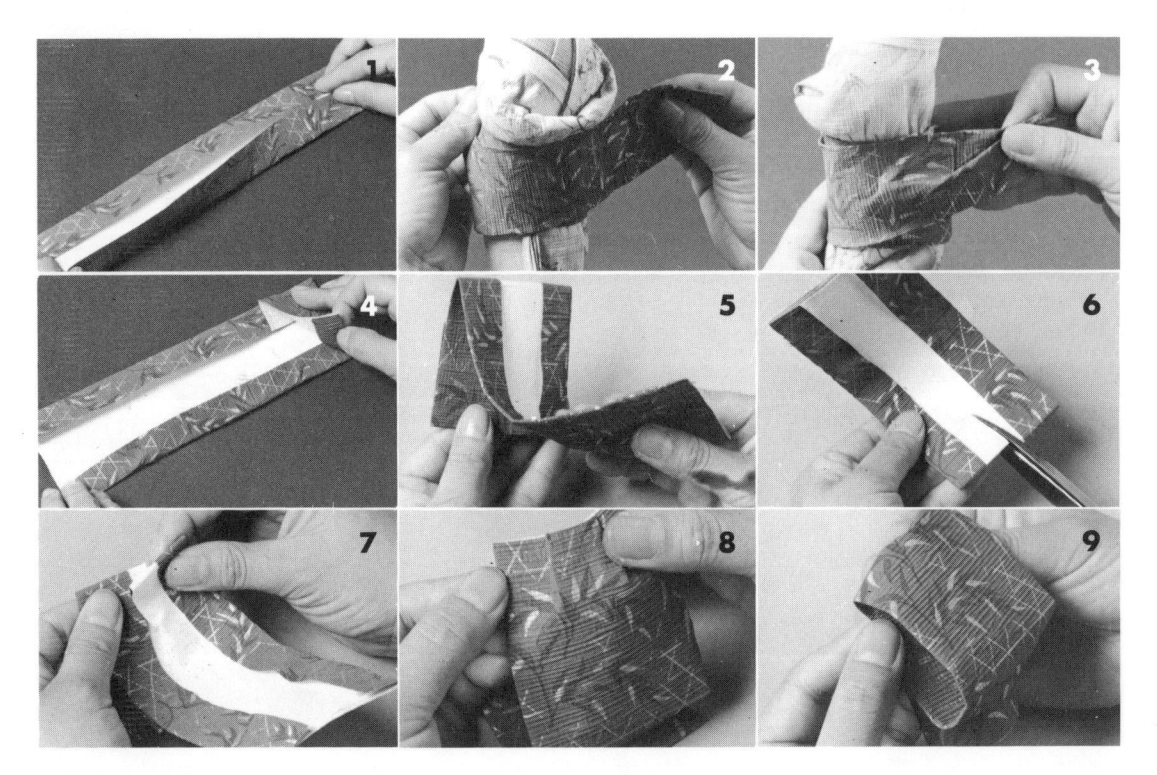

36

11. Turn it over to the front and make a tuck.
12. Turn it over to the back and glue the ends.
13. Put the side flaps through the drum.
14. Insert the tab of the drum in the front *obi* and glue. If it is unstable, put a string through and tie it so it cannot be seen.

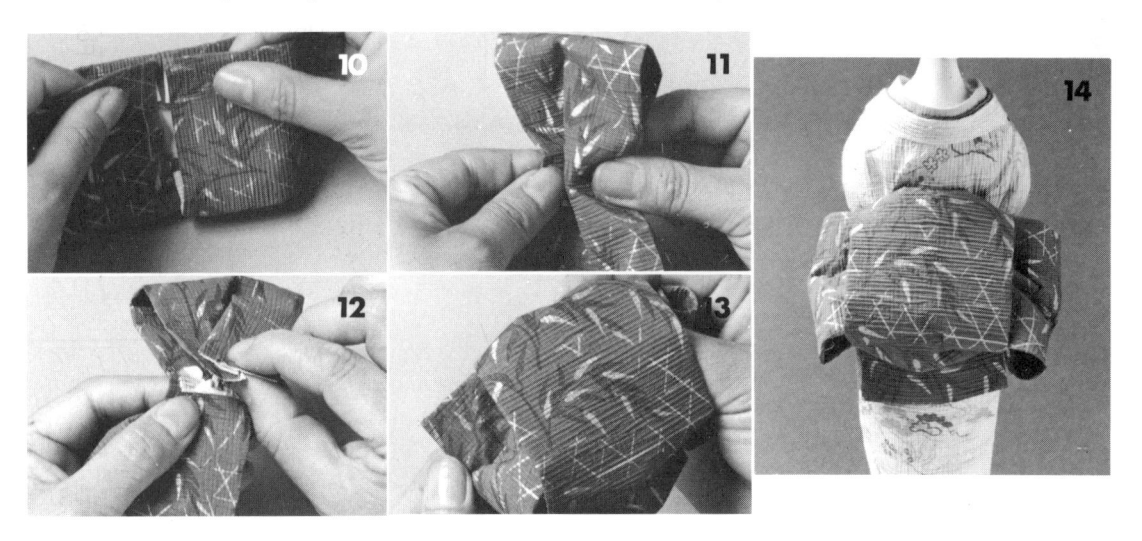

Oiran Obi (p. 15) ★

The *Oiran Obi* is a drum tied in front. The drum is slightly larger than the *Otaiko* style.

Materials:
1 piece of gathered paper with a print for the *obi* (21×25 cm.)
1 piece of drawing paper for the lining.

How to Make It
First, cut out the parts: front *obi* (10×16 cm.), drum (11×25 cm.), and side flaps (11×25 cm.) and line with drawing paper of the same size.

1. First, wrap the front *obi* around as you did with the drum style, but from the center back. Glue in front.
2. Fold the lined drum, make the tuck and shape it.
3. Fold the side flaps, make the tuck, put it through the drum and glue.
4. Insert the drum in the front *obi*.

BASIC POINT 4
HOW TO GATHER PAPER

No matter how beautiful a person is, that beauty is cut in half by messy hair. Dolls are the same. So for a beautiful coiffure, it is important how you gather the paper. Learn the essentials, and soon you will be able to make many hair styles.

Japanese paper has lines in it lengthwise. Place a stick perpendicular to the lines on the paper. Paper with a length of 20 cm. is the easiest to wind and gather.

Materials:
1 piece of black Japanese paper (18×20 cm.)
1 stick for gathering (one about the width of your ring finger is best.)
Notice: The long side of the paper will have the lines running lengthwise.

How to Make It
1. Start to wind the paper from one end with the stick.
2. Wind it carefully and not too tight. When you have finished, you should be able to slide the stick out.
3. With the stick inside, hold the paper down firmly and squeeze it from the center.
4. After squeezing the center, shift your hands gradually all over toward the center.
5. Squeeze the ends by pushing gently with your fingernails.
6. Next, take out the stick. Push the paper together gently like a spring.
7. Open the gathered paper and rewind with the stick from the opposite end. Wind it a little tighter than before.
8. Squeeze from the center as you did before.
9. You can squeeze the paper while turning the stick.
10. Take the stick out. Squeeze firmly by pushing in from both ends with your fingers.
11. Open the paper, stretch it with both hands and adjust the wrinkles.
12. Repeat the squeezing procedure from the opposite end.
13. Repeat 10–15 times. If carefully done, the curves will stand out, and the wrinkles will be deep.

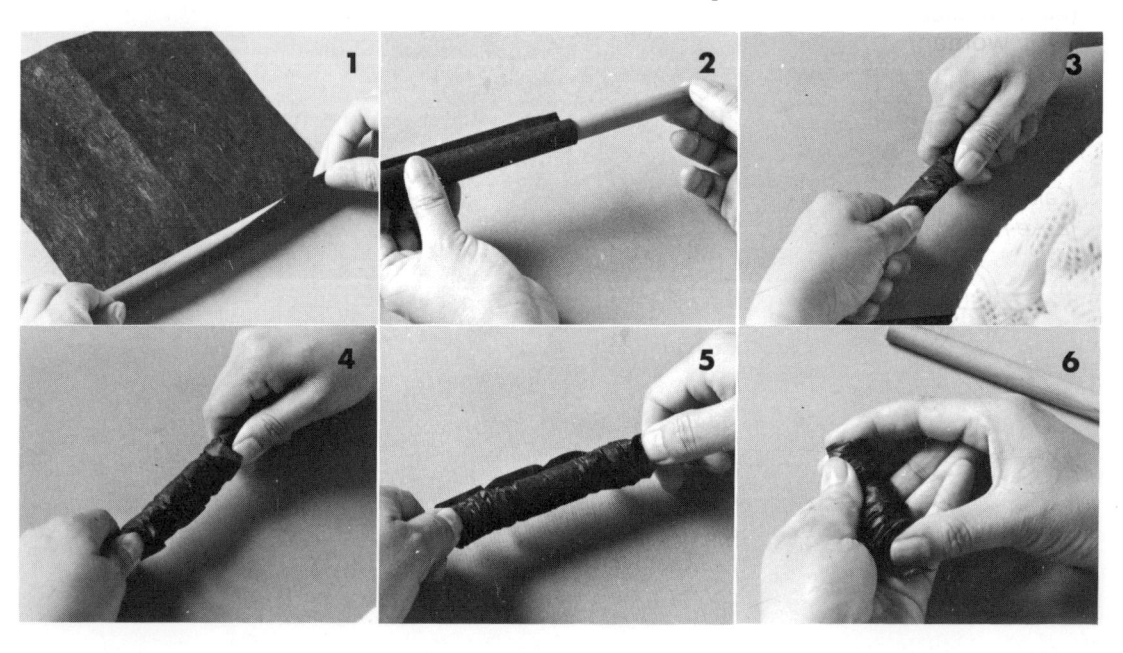

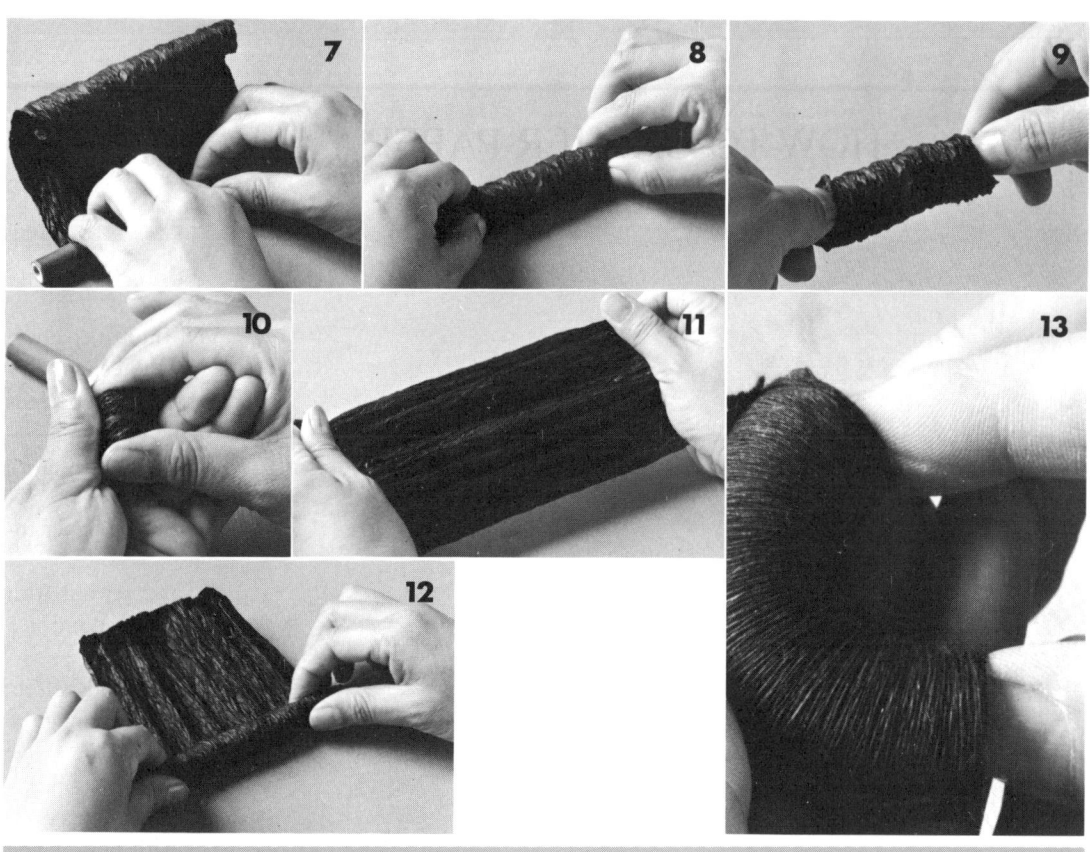

Various Kinds of Knots

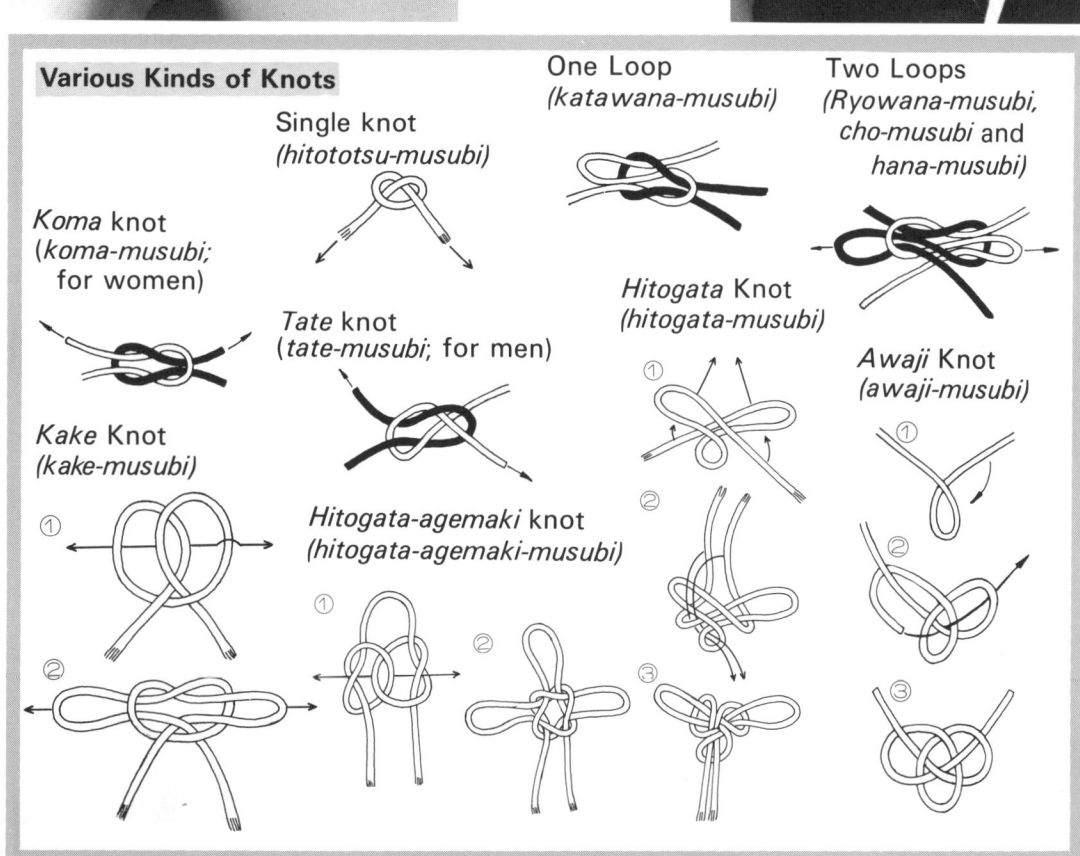

Koma knot
(*koma-musubi*;
for women)

Single knot
(*hitototsu-musubi*)

One Loop
(*katawana-musubi*)

Two Loops
(*Ryowana-musubi*,
cho-musubi and
hana-musubi)

Tate knot
(*tate-musubi*; for men)

Hitogata Knot
(*hitogata-musubi*)

Awaji Knot
(*awaji-musubi*)

Kake Knot
(*kake-musubi*)

Hitogata-agemaki knot
(*hitogata-agemaki-musubi*)

39

BASIC POINT 5
HAIR STYLE

The hair styles are divided into two kinds: wigs —the little girl's short bob, three year-old boy's style, ponytail, etc., and the tied up styles—styles with the forelock and back hair joined together, children's styles, men's styles, etc. Since black gathered paper is used for all styles, learn the essentials of paper gathering and then go on the hair styles.

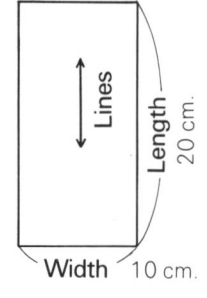

Lines
Length 20 cm.
Width 10 cm.

(1) Wigs

When using the wig styles, first make the head, body and clothes.

(a) Basic Short Bob Style (p. 10)

The most basic wig style is the little girl's short bob. To make it easier for you, the *kimono* is not on yet.

Materials:
  1 piece of black gathered Japanese paper for the back hair (18×20 cm.)
  1 piece of the same for the forelock (7×10 cm.)
  String.
  1 child's body.

How to Make It
  1. Make the back hair. Unroll 8 cm. of the paper, starting from the end rolled last.
  2. Put string through the part still rolled.
  3. Tie in a knot, leaving the ends as they are.
  4. Adjust the wrinkles near the knot and pull the hair back in the direction of the wrinkles.
  5. Cut off the ends of the string. Turn the paper

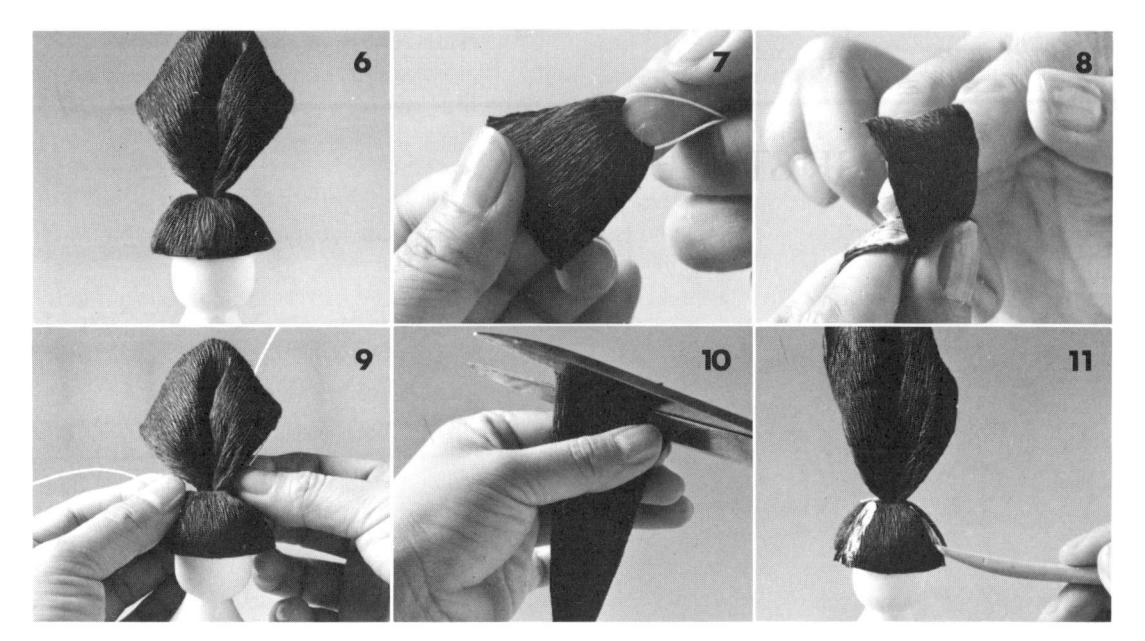

over and pull out the loops. Join and glue.
6. Bring the joined part forward, put it on the head and glue.
7. Make the forelock. Fold the paper for the forelock in two and put a string through it. Pull it and hold down the wrinkles.
8. Next, put glue between the folded parts. Shape it so it will fit on the forehead easily.
9. Put the forelock on over the place where the back hair was joined. Put it on the forehead. After cutting the length, glue it and tie it with string going through the forelock. Cut off the ends of the string.
10. Cut the ends of the back hair evenly.
11. Put glue on both sides of the forelock.
12. Fold both ends of the back hair to the inside 5 mm. Bring it down along the head and glue to the forelock.
13. Holding the end of the back hair, spread out the wrinkles and let it flow naturally.
14. Next put a little glue on the temples.
15. Put the hair against the face and push in at the temples with your fingers.
16. Now you have finished the short bob style.

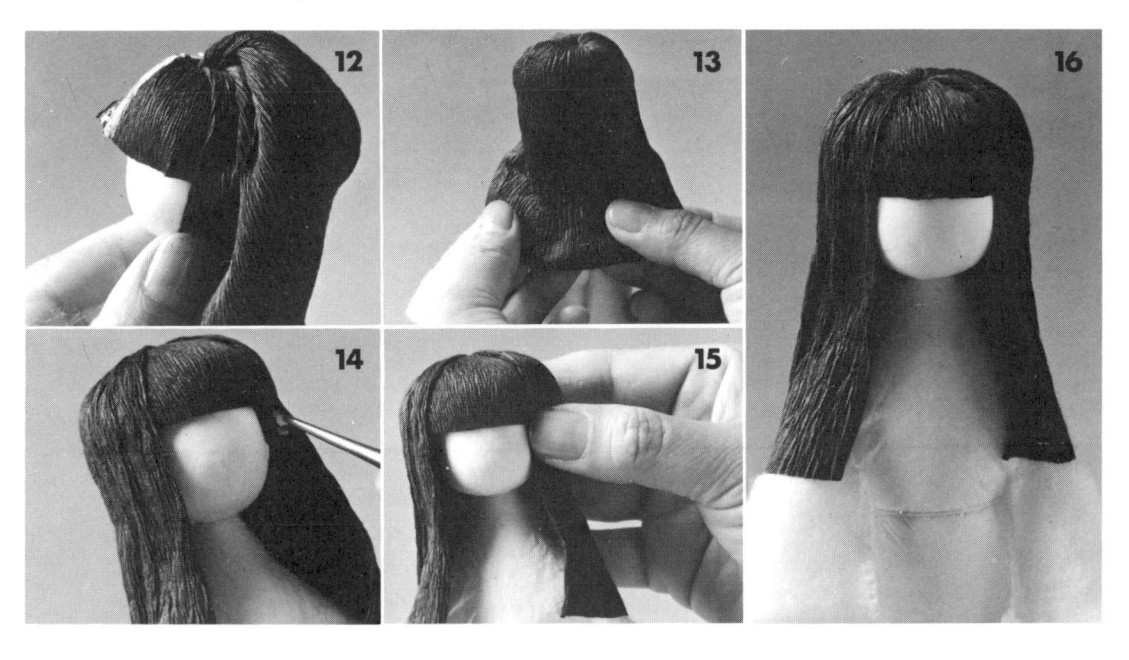

● **Variations of the Short Bob—put on a chignon.**

Dress the body and put on a decorative chignon or bow. It will make the short bob even cuter. Variations 2 and 3 are those put on adults. See the tied up styles in the adults' hairstyle section.

★ **Variation 1. Bow**

Make it with a cute colored ribbon. Since it is small, make it with leftover paper.

Materials:
1 piece of pink gathered paper (4×6 cm.)
A little cotton.

How to Make It
1. Wrap a little cotton in the paper. Fold it in three places. Bring the ends together at the center and glue.
2. Cut a long, narrow piece of paper for the knot of the bow. Put it in the middle and shape the bow.
3. Twist the ends of the knot with your fingers and glue it stationary. Cut off the ends 1 cm. from the knot.
4. Insert the ends in the short bob.

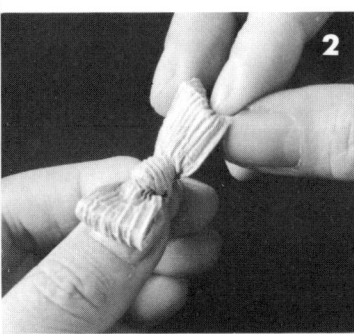

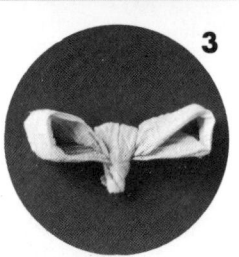

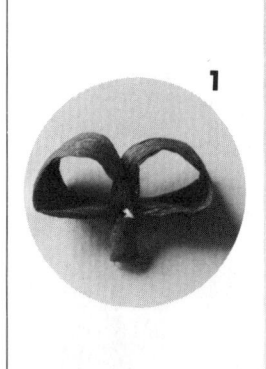

★ **Variation 2. The *Chigo* Topknot**

Materials:
1 piece of black gathered Japanese paper (5×20 cm.)
A little more paper cut long and narrow.
String.

How to Make It
1. See p. 51 and make the *Chigo* loops.
2. Insert on top of the short bob and decorate it with little flowers.

★ **Variation 3.** *Momoware*

Materials:
1 piece of black gathered Japanese paper for the chignon (8×20 cm.)
A little more paper cut long and narrow.
1 piece of pink gathered paper for the chignon band (6×10 cm.) / String.

How to Make It
1. See p. 50 and make the *Momoware* chignon.
2. Insert on top of the short bob and decorate with a floral hairpin.

★ **Variation 4. Boy Doll's Style**
The boy doll's style is the young man's topknot put on the short bob. For the girl doll just put small *Chigo* loops.

Materials:
1 piece of black gathered Japanese paper for the back hair (18×20 cm.)
1 piece of the same for the forelock (7×20 cm.)
1 piece of the same for the topknot (10× 20 cm.) / String.
1 standard size child's body.

How to Make It
First, put on the back hair and forelock of the short bob.

1. Wind the paper for the topknot around a stick 8 mm. in diameter. Leave 6 cm. of the paper unrolled. Take the stick out, put string through and tie.
2. Tie it tightly and cut off the ends of the string. Next, pull the unroleld 6 cm. back firmly (sidelocks) and fold on three places.
3. Bring back the ends of the loops. Put string around from underneath and cross it over.
4. Place a stick under the topknot and bring it up over the back hair. Tie the crossed string in a knot.
5. Cut off the ends so the topknot is slightly longer than the back hair.
6. Cut the forelock of the short bob in a widow's peak and glue on the topknot.

* For the young man's topknot, put this topknot on the hair style base.

43

(b) Three Year-Old Boy

Materials:
- 1 piece of black gathered Japanese paper for the hair and sidelocks (8×20 cm.)
- 1 yellow narrow decorative string.
- 1 standard size little boy's body.

How to Make It

1. Wind a piece of black gathered paper on a stick, leaving 8 cm. unwound. Put string through the wound part and tie. Cut off 4 cm. of the unwound 8 cm. to make the two sidelocks.
2. Pull the remaining 4 cm. up. Adjust the shape and tie with string, making a bow at the root.
3. Next, open the part at the root, put on 2 cm. of glue and fold lengthwise. Cut to an adequate length.
4. Make the sidelocks from the paper cut in Step 1. Apply glue and fold lengthwise three times.
5. Next, shape it while closing the ends.
6. Tie in the center with string.
7. Put the hair on the head. Glue the sidelocks on at one end only.

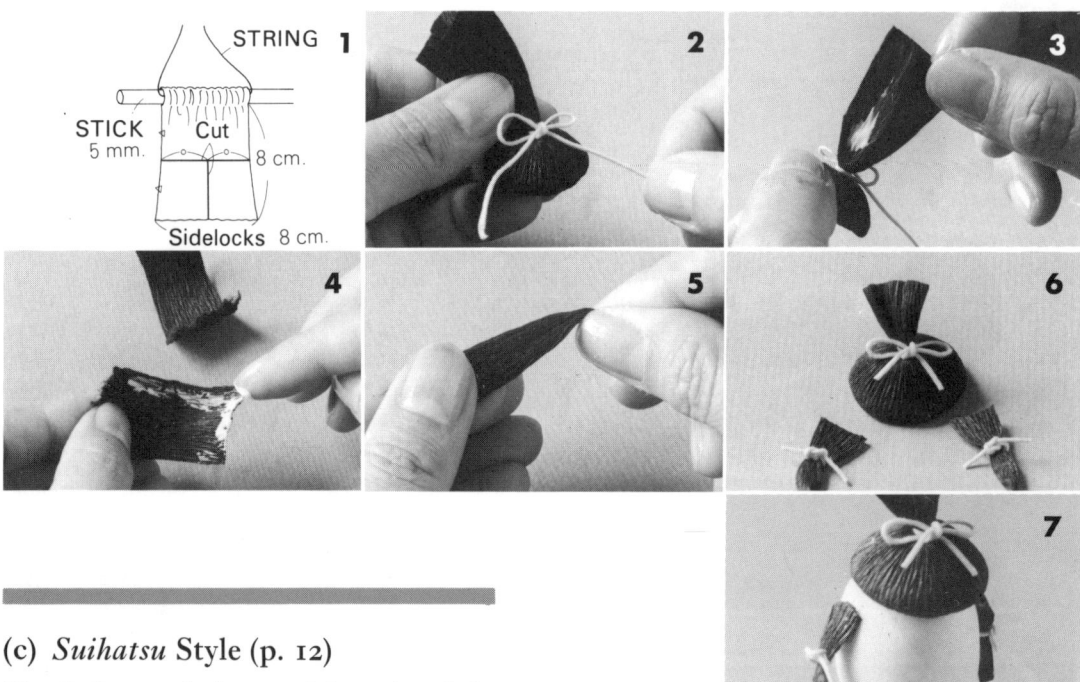

(c) *Suihatsu* Style (p. 12)

The *Suihatsu* style is one of the styles of the *Azuchi* and *Momoyama* Periods (about 400 years ago). It is a beautiful style using the natural flow of the hair. Use paper with good wrinkles.

Materials:
- 1 piece of black gathered Japanese paper for the back hair (20 cm. sq.)
- 1 piece of the same for the forelock (10×20 cm.)
- 1 piece of the same for the hair hanging down the back (5×20 cm.)
- A little more of the same paper.
- 1 piece of thick white Japanese paper for the wide string.
- String.

How to Make It

First, make the adult's body. Make the head the same as the one for the short bob up to the neck, then make the body (see p. 25.) There will be no chignon, so do not lengthen the legs.

1. Put on the *kimono*. Use the *hoso-obi* and tie it in front.
2. Wind the paper for the back hair on a stick 1.4 cm. in diameter, leaving 8 cm. unwound. Take out the stick, put string through and tie.
3. Tie the string, leaving a hole big enough for

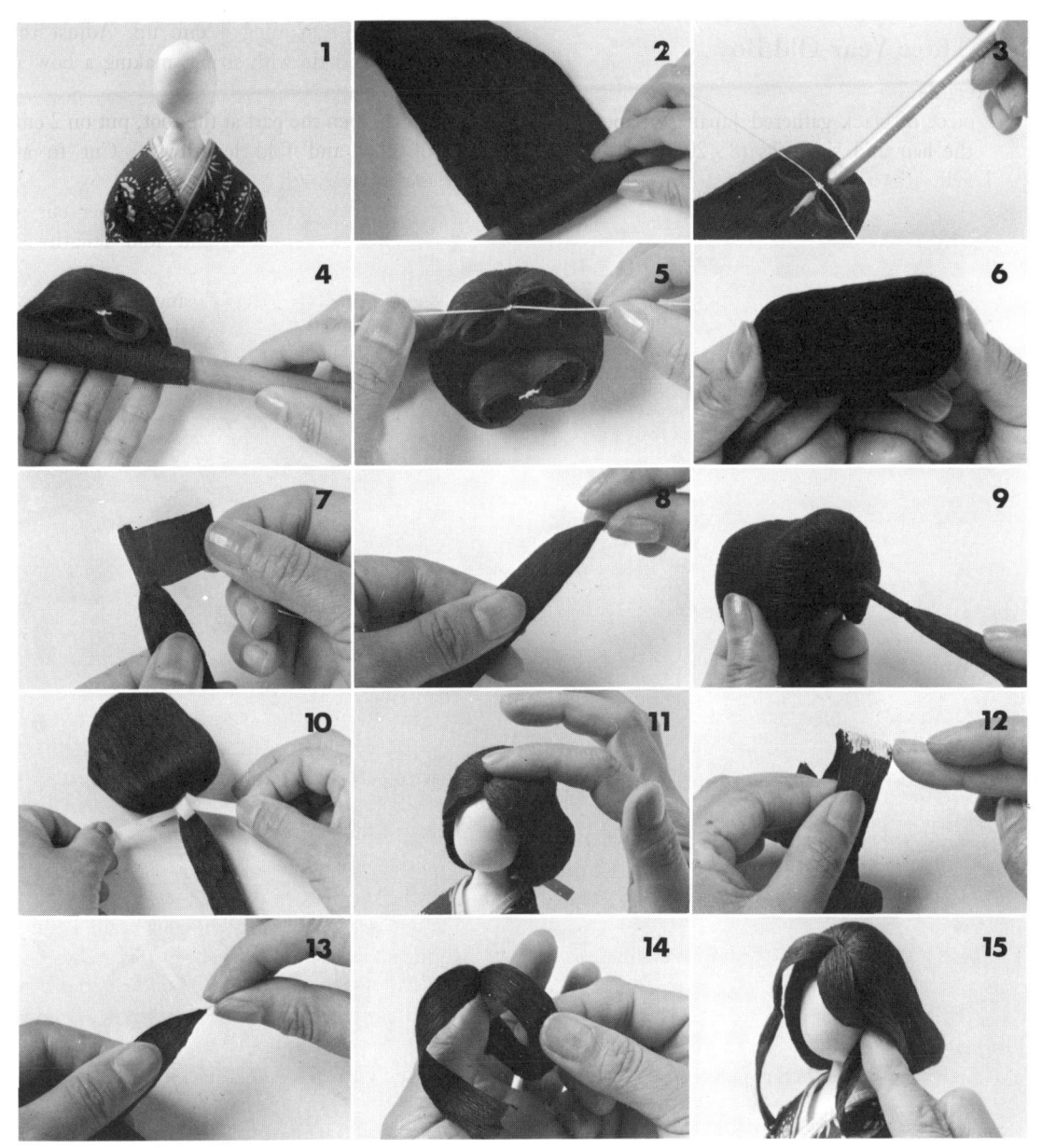

a pencil to pass through.
4. Next, wind the other end around the stick.
5. Put the string through likewise and tie loosely. Do not leave much of a hole. This will be the top of the head.
6. Hold both knots and adjust the wrinkles.
7. Make the hair hanging down in the back. First, fold the paper for that part in three lengthwise and glue. Close one end and wind the 2×5 cm. piece of paper around it. This will be inserted.
8. Next, put glue on the other end.
9. Insert the first end in the hole left open and glue.
10. Put the wide string around the base and tie in a knot.
11. Adjust the back hair and put glue on the top of the head. Put the hair on and secure it.
12. Next, make the forelock. First, fold the paper for the forelock in two widthwise. Put glue on the loop.
13. Make the part to be inserted by twisting the glued place with your fingers.
14. Make the ends hang down on the right and left.
15. Insert it in the center of the top of the head and glue it. Bring down around the face and shape it.

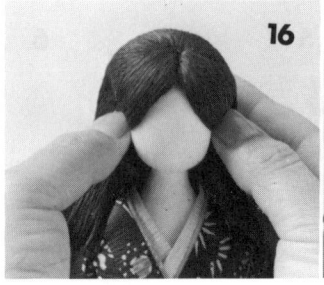

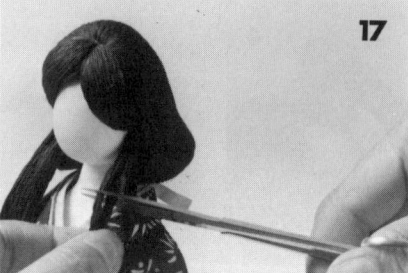

16. Hold the forelocks down by the ears and glue.
17. Cut to an adequate length, and then make lengthwise cuts in the ends of the forelock, which will make fringed sidelocks.

(2) Tied Up Hair Styles

In making the tied up styles, you must put the base of the style on when making the head. Presented are women's styles with chignons, children's styles, and young men and *samurai*'s styles.

(a) Woman's Hairdo

Base of the tied up style—with the back hair and forelock joined.
The base of the woman's tied up style is different from the child's only in size. Try to make many.

Materials:
1 piece of black gathered Japanese paper for the back hair (20 cm. sq.)
1 piece of the same for the forelock (6×20 cm.)
2 pieces of thin white Japanese paper (1× 10 cm.)
String.
1 standard size neckless woman's head.

How to Make It
1. First, make the back hair. Wind the paper for it around a stick, leaving 6 cm. for the border of the back hair. Put string through and tie, leaving a hole the width of a pencil.
2. Insert the side that will be the top of the head in the back hair.
3. Insert it so the center of the back of the head meets the string's knot.
4. Next, make the forelock. Wind the paper for it on a stick, leaving 8 cm. Tie it with string.
5. Insert it in the back hair with the forelock facing the front of the face.
6. Open the inserted ends and wrap with the paper for the border of the back hair (together with the paper for the face).
7. Bring it down from the top of the head and wind with paper tape at a place about $2/3$ the length of the face. Glue.
8. Make the border of the back hair full and round so it will lie along the head. Apply glue and put it on the back of the head.
9. Wind the border of the back hair and the area under the chin together with paper tape and glue.
10. Shape the back hair. Glue the forelock and both sides of the back hair to the face.

Now you have made the base for the woman's hairdo. After this, do the body (p. 25) and *kimono* (p. 34) and then add the chignon. Lengthen the body in proportion to the height of the chignon. First, decide what doll you want to make and then do it up to the *kimono*.

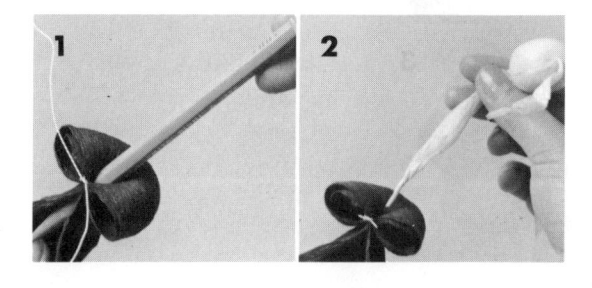

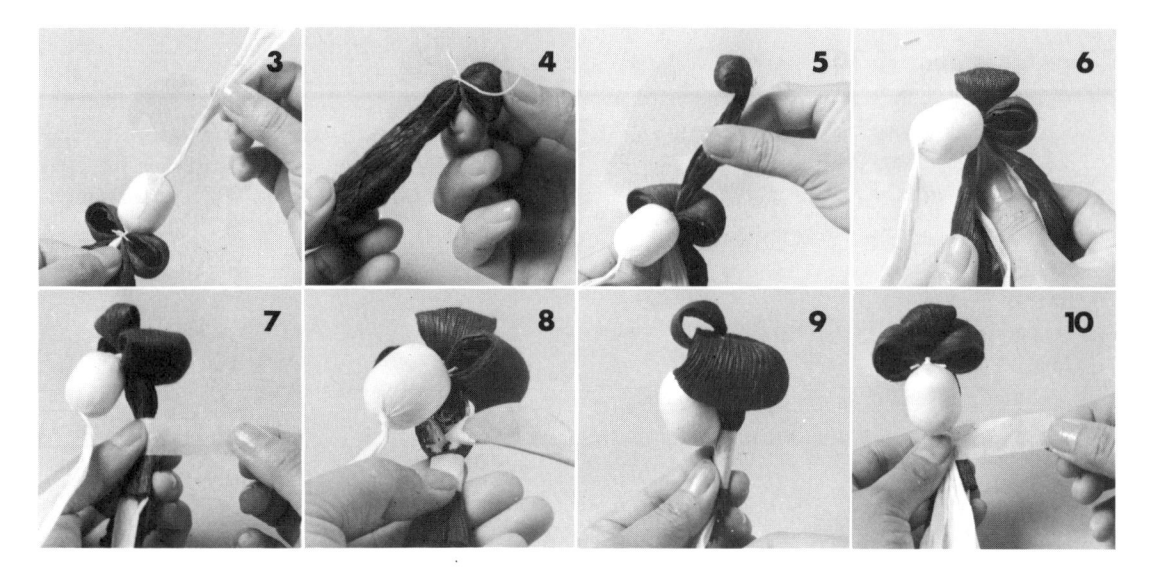

Variations of the Adult's Hair

Make the body for the coiffured head, then put on the *kimono* and the chignon. Beginners try many different chignons.

Tachi-hyogo (p. 16) ★

This is one of the chignons that were popular among the courtesans in the *Setsu-hyogo* district (western part of Japan). If the forelock does not match the size of the face, make fringed forelocks.

Materials:
1 piece of black gathered Japanese paper for the chignon (8×25 cm.)
1 little cotton.
1 ornamental hairpin.
1 dressed adult's body.

How to Make It
1. Put a thin piece of cotton (1.5×15 cm.) in the paper for the chignon. Fold in three lengthwise and glue.
2. Fold in two widthwise, leaving one end 5 cm. longer than the other. With the short end as the axis, wind the long end around once and tie.
3. Adjust the knot while pulling down.
4. Cut the part to be inserted to a length of 2.5 cm.
5. Next, insert the ornamental hairpin. Wind the remaining black paper around the ends and glue.
6. Insert the ends in the hole in the back hair.
7. For reference: Make fringed forelocks by making lengthwise cuts long, thin pieces of black Japanese paper.

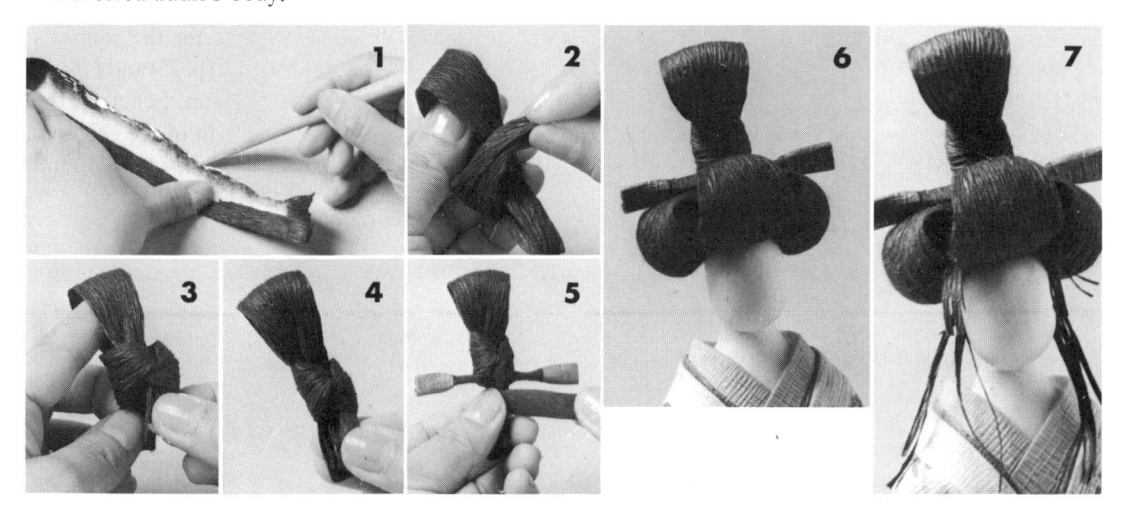

Shimada Chignon (p. 14) ★

This style became popular among the courtesans in *Shimada* (one of the stages on the *Tokaido* highway) in the late *Edo* Period. There are many kinds, such as the *Bunkin Takashimada*, the *Tsubushi Shimada* of the *geisha*, etc.

Materials:
   1 piece of black gathered Japanese paper for the front chignon (10×20 cm.)
   1 piece of the same for the back chignon (7×20 cm.)
   1 more piece of the same (1×5 cm.)
   String.
   A miniature wide string, comb, ornamental hairpin, floral hairpin, etc.

How to Make It
   1. Leave 2 cm. as the ends. Put string through and tie. Leave enough space for the back chignon to be inserted. Do not cut off the ends of the string.
   2. Likewise, leave 4 cm. as the ends of the back chignon and tie. Make it round.
   3. Insert the back chignon in the front one.
   4. Bring the string of the front chignon around and tie the back one. Cut off the ends.
   5. Wind the 1×5 cm. piece of paper around the chignon ends.
   6. Tie with the wide string.
   7. Decorate with a comb and floral pin.

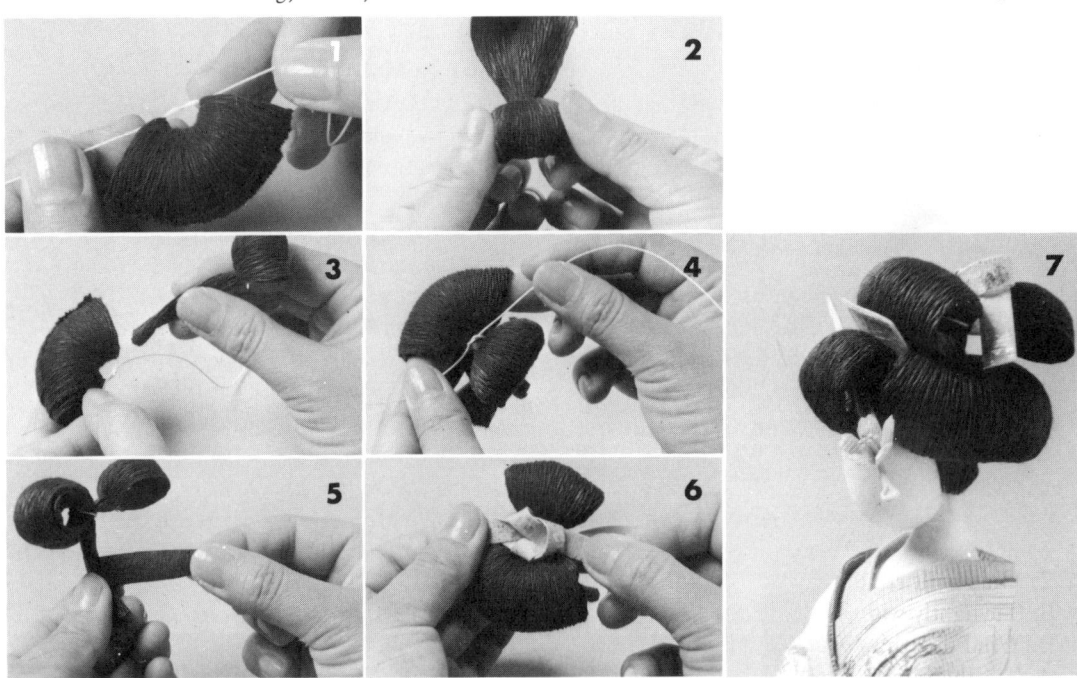

Taka-shimada (p. 14) ★

This is representative of a bride's style. Add miniature decorations.

Materials:
   1 piece of black gathered Japanese paper for the chignon (10×30 cm.)
   1 other piece of black Japanese paper (2×5 cm.)
   1 piece of thin white Japanese paper (1.5×5 cm.)
   A little cotton. / String.
   A miniature comb, floral hairpin, and *takenaga* (made of lined gathered paper (1×17 cm.) folded in three.)

How to Make It
   1. Fold the paper for the chignon in two and put string through the loop. Put a thin piece of cotton in the loop.

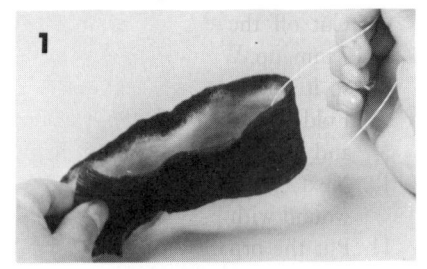

48

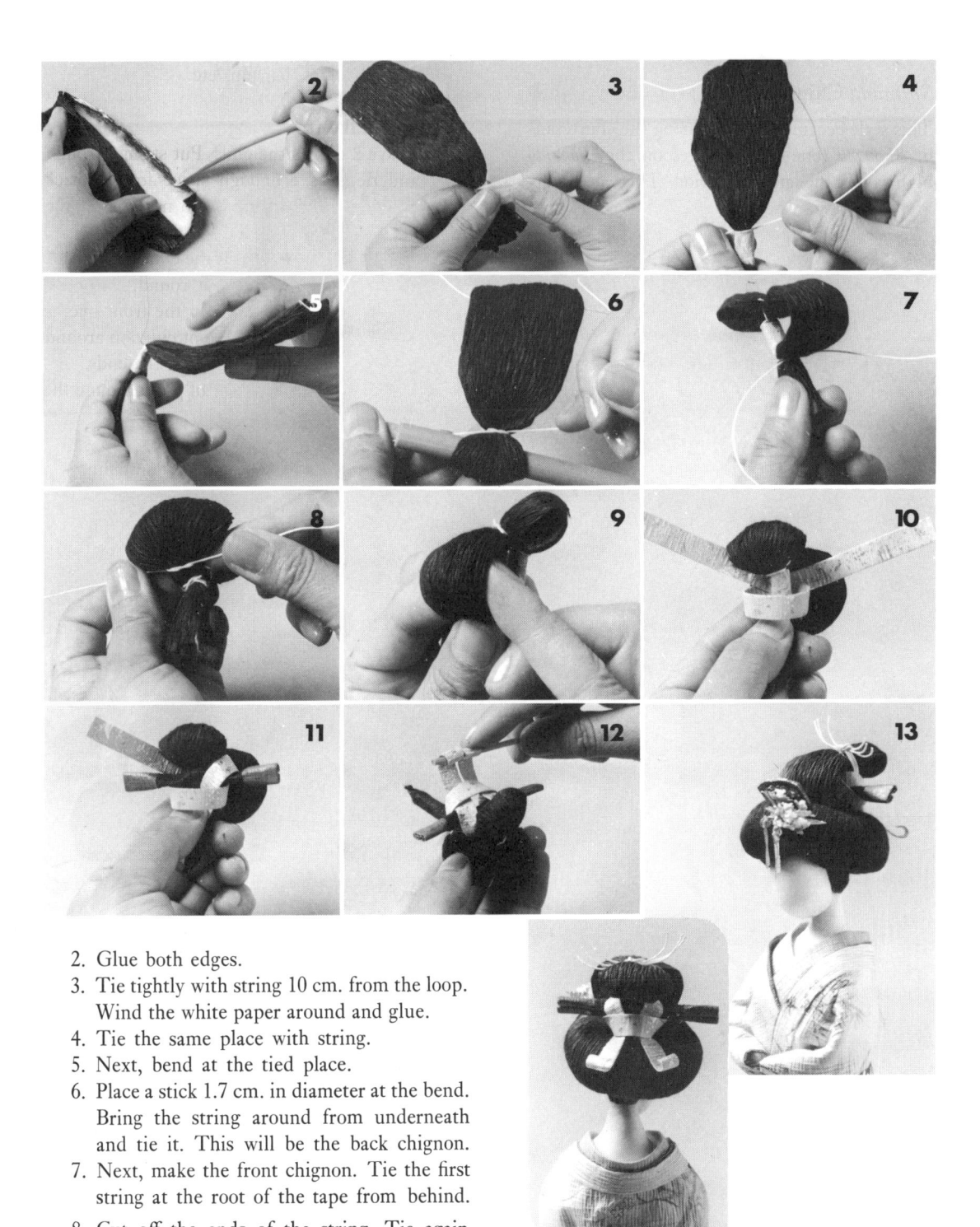

2. Glue both edges.
3. Tie tightly with string 10 cm. from the loop. Wind the white paper around and glue.
4. Tie the same place with string.
5. Next, bend at the tied place.
6. Place a stick 1.7 cm. in diameter at the bend. Bring the string around from underneath and tie it. This will be the back chignon.
7. Next, make the front chignon. Tie the first string at the root of the tape from behind.
8. Cut off the ends of the string. Tie again 7 mm. up. Wrap black paper around the ends so it can be easily inserted.
9. Fold the ends of the front chignon in 5 mm. and shape.
10. Next, put the *takenaga* through the place wound with paper and cross the ends inside.
11. Put the ornamental hairpin through.
12. Curl the ends of the *takenaga* with a toothpick and insert them in the hole in the back hair.
13. Put the comb and floral hairpin in. Put decorative string on the knots of the front and back chignons.

49

Momoware (p. 15) ★

This is a style that was popular among teenagers in the *Meiji* and *Taisho* Periods. There are many ways to make it, but the easiest is by making cuts.

Materials:
1 piece of black gathered Japanese paper for the chignon (16×20 cm.) / String.
A miniature chignon band made of 1 piece of gathered paper with a print (7×20 cm.)
A fringed hairpin (p. 58), round hairpin, etc.

How to Make It
First, wind the paper for the chignon on a stick 1.7 cm. in diameter. Leave ends of 2 cm. Put string through and tie. Leave the ends of the string uncut.
1. Cut the center of the loops, making two parts.
2. Fold the paper for the chignon band lenghthwise in three. Bring it through both loops.
3. Gently twist the ends of the band and insert in the front loops. Tie with string and cut off the ends.
4. Wind the ends of the chignon with black paper.
5. Insert it in the back hair and forelock and decorate.

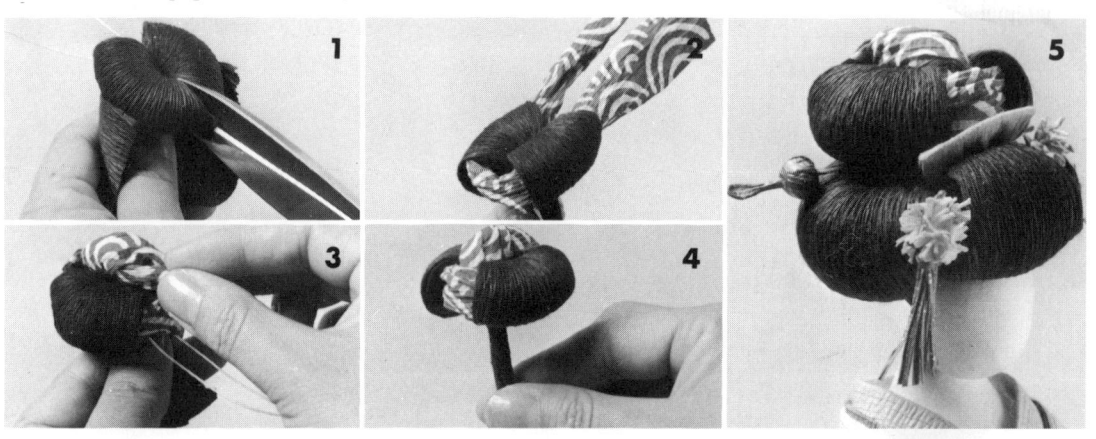

Marumage (p. 13) ★

This is the style of a married woman. Put on simple ornaments. Usually a young wife uses a a red chignon band and an older woman uses a blue one.

Materials:
1 piece of black gathered Japanese paper for the chignon (10×20 cm.)
1 other piece of black Japanese paper (2× 5 cm.) / String. / A hairpin.

How to Make It
1. Wind the paper for the chignon on a stick 2.5 cm. in diameter. Leave ends of 2.5 cm. Put string through and tie.
2. Cut off the ends of the string. Fold both ends of the chignon 5 mm. and shape.
3. Put the hairpin through. Wind black paper around the ends. Insert it in the hair. When you put on the chignon band, hold it in place with the hairpin. (See the *Shimada* chignon band, p. 48.)

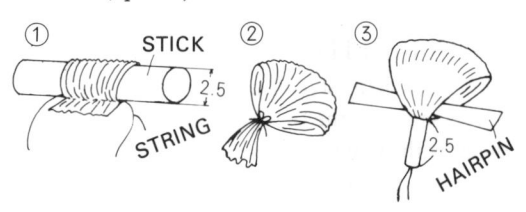

Oiran Style (p. 15) ★

Try the *oiran* hairdo after getting used to making the others. It is also called the *Yokohyogo* chignon. Put it on a full hairdo.

Materials:
1 piece of black gathered Japanese paper for the chignon (10×30 cm.)
1 piece of the same (5×20 cm.)
1 other piece of black Japanese paper (2× 5 cm.) / A little cotton. / String.
A miniature comb, hairpin, thick decorative string with a tassel, etc.

How to Make It
1. First, fold the big paper for the chignon in two.
2. With a stick wind it from both ends to the center. Squeeze the paper and pull the stick out.
3. Tie with string.
4. Next, tie the four ends of the string together.
5. Put a thin piece of cotton 5 cm. long in the small black piece of paper.
6. Fold the paper in three with the cotton inside. Put it around the center of the chignon and cut off the ends 5 cm. down.
7. Wrap paper around the ends and glue.
8.9. Insert in the hole in the back hair and decorate.

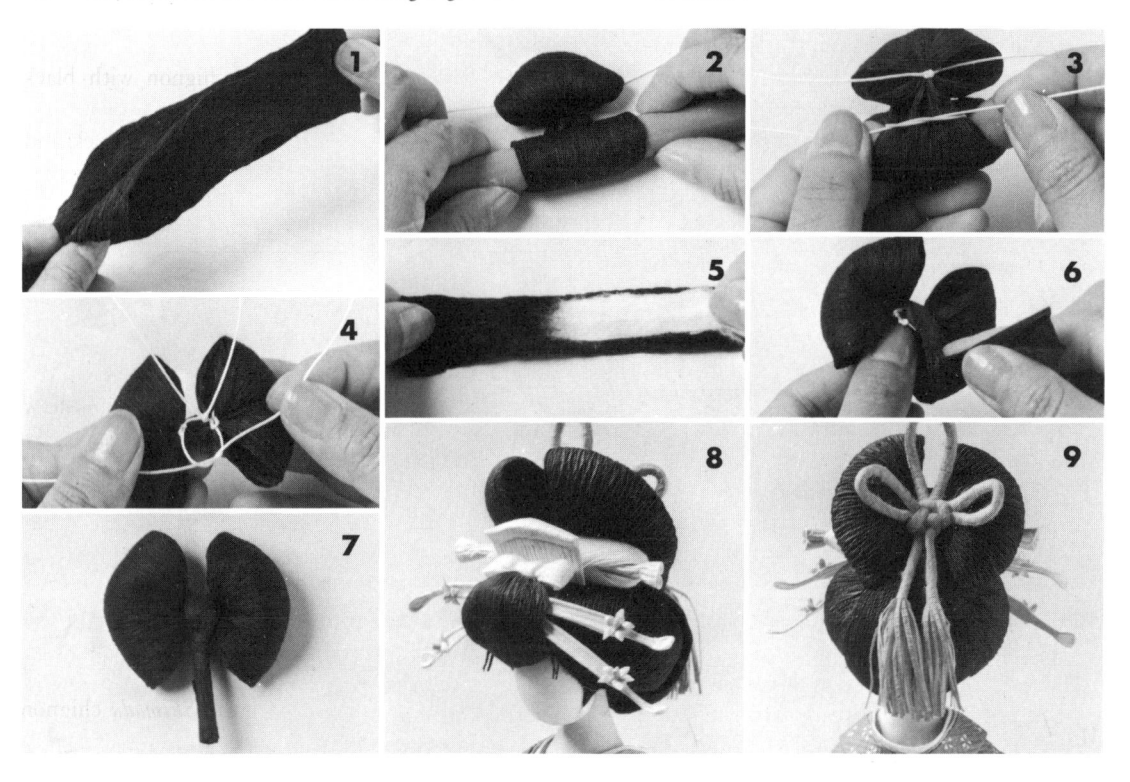

(b) Child's Hair Style

The basic hair style of the *chigo* and *kamuro* is the same as the adult's, only smaller. Make them with a piece of black gathered Japanese paper for the forelock (6×20 cm.) and another for the back hair (18×20 cm.) (See p. 46.)

Chigo-mage ═══════════════════★

Materials:
　1 piece of black gathered Japanese paper for the chignon (5×20 cm.)
　1 piece of the same (gathered or ungathered) (2.5×6 cm.)
　A little cotton. / String.
　Miniature floral decorations.

How to Make It
1. Put a thin piece of cotton in the paper for the chignon, fold it in three and glue.
2. Fold in half widthwise with the glued part inside. Tie at the fold.
3. Use a stick 1.5 cm. in diameter to make two loops at the center. Tie tightly with the remaining string.

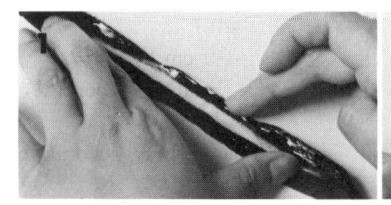

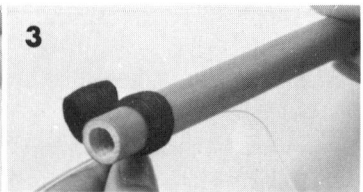

4. Wind the small piece of paper around the ends of the paper and string. Cut off at a length of 2.5 cm.
5. Insert it in the back hair. Decorate with fringed forelocks (see sketch) and floral hairpins.

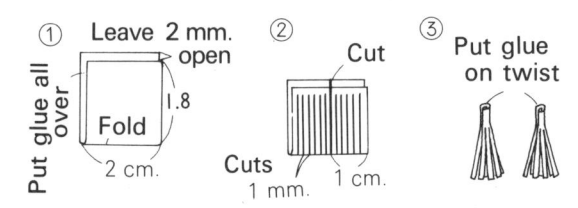

Kamuro (p. 15) ★

This is the hair style of the little girls who helped the courtesans. Decorate it with bows of three colors, etc.

Materials:
 1 piece of black gathered Japanese paper for the chignon (5×20 cm.)
 A little more black Japanese paper for the fringed forelocks and sidelocks.
 2 pieces of thin white Japanese paper (1× 5 cm.)
 String.
 1 piece each of 6 cm. sq. gathered paper in red, purple and yellow.
 Narrow string in the same three colors.
 1 red and one purple string with tassles.
 A comb, 10 flowers, 2 fringed hairpins, 3 gold paper bells (See p. 59).
 1 dressed child's body with a red *kimono* and a black *obi*.

How to Make It
First, make the bows. (See sketches 1–3.)

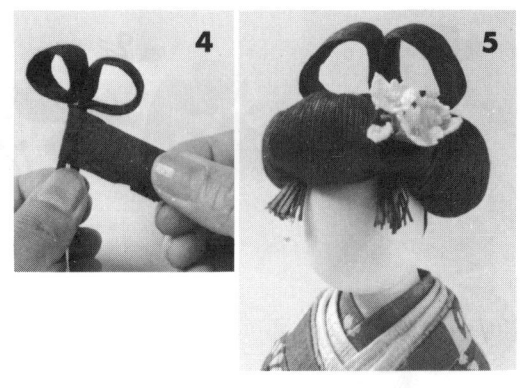

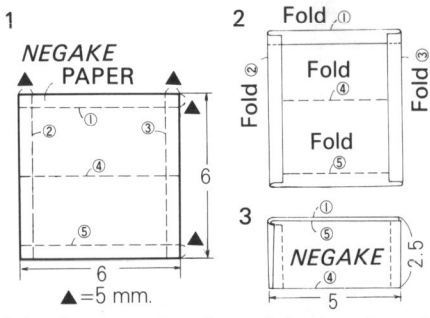

1. Make the paper into bows by tying them in the center with regular string.
2. Overlap the bows one on top of the other with the yellow one on top, then red and purple. Tie them securely with string.
3. Put a thin piece of cotton 3 cm. long in the chignon paper. Fold in three lengthwise and glue. Put glue only on the part where the cotton is.
4. Fold in half widthwise and place a stick 5 mm. in diameter in the fold. Tie string around the paper close to the stick.
5. Pull the stick out. Wind white paper around one end of the paper and both ends of the string and glue.
6. Put the chignon over the bows.

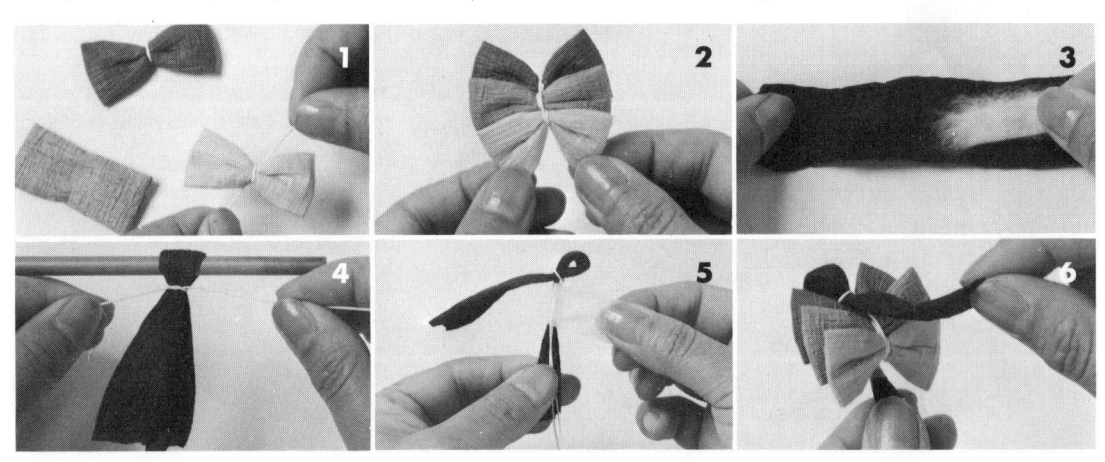

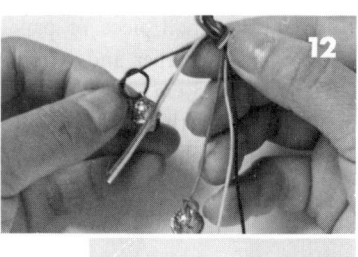

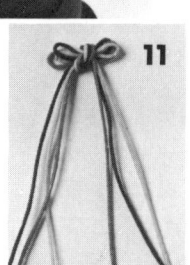

7. Wind white paper around the ends and the string. Cut to a length of 2.5 cm.
8. Insert the chignon in the base hair. Make fringed sidelocks and forelocks and put them on.
9. Next, insert the comb and put the flowers on it.
10. Put the fringed hairpins on both sides of the forelock. Glue the two tasseled strings on the forelock and on top of the chignon.
11. Put the three colored strings together and tie in a bow. (See p. 39.)
12. Tie bells on the ends.
13. Glue the bows with the bells on the cuffs.

(c) Men's Styles

Samurai's topknot (p. 10) ★

This is a topknot with the back hair done up. Use a young man's body. It is important that the wrinkles on the gathered paper be nice because no other decorations are used.

Materials:
1 piece of black gathered Japanese paper for the back hair (10×20 cm.)
2 pieces of the same for the sidelocks (5×20 cm.)
1 piece for the forelock (4×20 cm.)
String. / 1 young man's body.

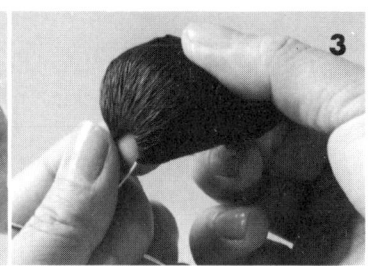

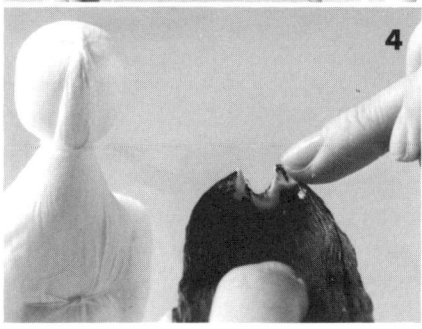

How to Make It
1. Fold the paper for the back hair in half and put string along the fold.
2. Glue together by putting glue along the fold about 2 cm. on the inside.
3. Before the glue dries, draw both ends of the string and shape it in a small half circle.
4. Cut off the ends of the string at the edge of the paper. Put a little glue on the inside of the paper.

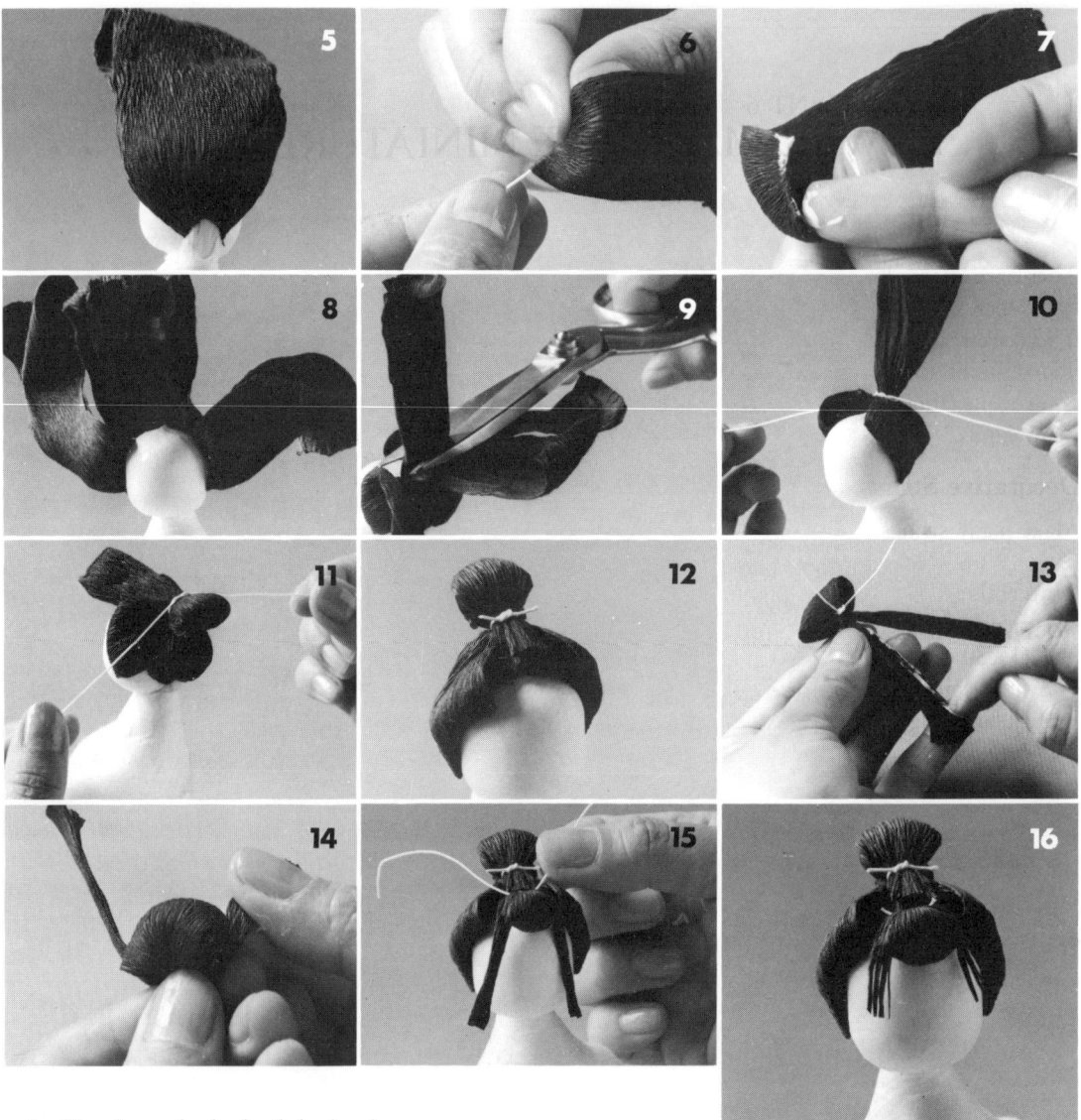

5. Glue it on the back of the head.
6. Next, make the sidelocks. Fold the paper in half widthwise and put string along the fold. Do the same as with the back hair, but do not draw the string so much. Shape it so it will fit the face. Make right and left side locks.
7.8. Put a little glue on the inside of the sidelocks and put them on both sides of the face.
9. Cut the inside piece of the back hair paper the length of the face. Do likewise with the sidelocks.
10. Bring both the back hair and sidelocks together on top of the head and tie with string. Leave the ends of the paper as they are.
11. Make the back topknot by bending all three pieces back and then forward. Tie with the same string. Cut off the ends of the string.
12. Adjust. Cut off the ends of the paper 2 cm. from the knot.
13. Leaving ends 5 cm. long, tie string around the paper for the forelocks to make a loop. Next, cut the ends in half lengthwise to make fringed forelocks. Fold the forelocks in three lengthwise and glue.
14. Twist the fringed forelocks once at the knot. Glue to the forelock.
15. Glue the forelock on the forehead. Cut off the ends of the fringed forelock.
16. Make lengthwise cuts in the fringed forelocks.

BASIC POINT 6
HOW TO MAKE THE MINIATURE ITEMS

There are many kinds of miniature items for dolls, such as hair decorations, implements, etc. There are ready made ones, but those you make yourself suit this kind of doll. The following is an explanation for beginners of how to make many kinds.

Decorative String ★

Make many strings of various kinds and colors.

Materials:
1 piece of gathered paper in a color you like (1×30 cm.)
A little cotton.
Regular string.

How to Make It
● **Thin string** (the same thickness as regular string)
1. Put glue on the paper.
2. Put one piece of regular string lengthwise down the middle of the paper and move it around in the glue.
3. Fold the paper in half lengthwise and make line along the string with your fingernail.
4. Cut along the line.
5. Smooth down the cut edge and roll the string.
6. Do this by rolling it on a flat surface with your palms. Put some paper with a rough surface underneath if it slides too much.

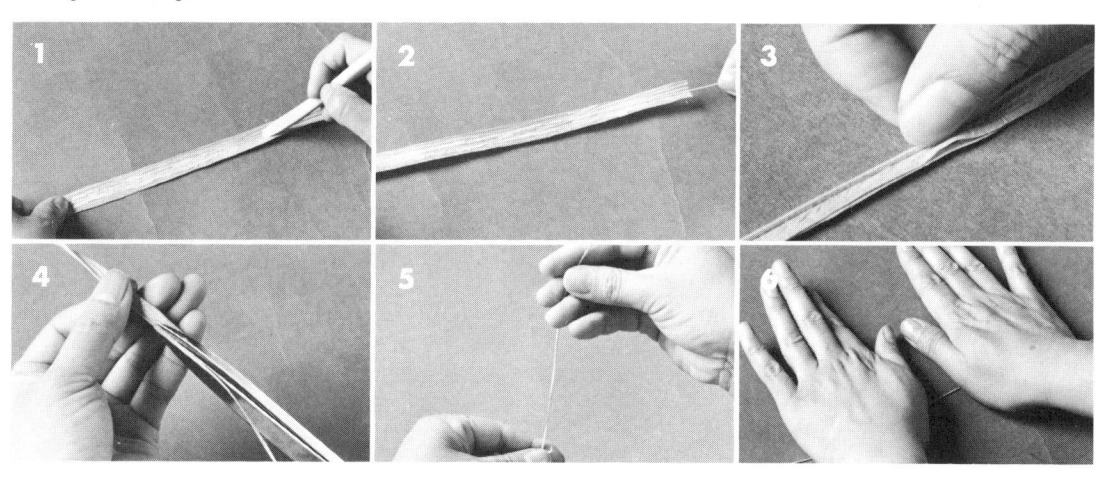

● **Thick string**
Make it the same way as the thin one, but wrap cotton in it for extra thickness. You can also make bows and arrows, swords, sticks, flutes, etc. this way.
1. Put glue on a piece of regular string and wind cotton around it. Make sure the cotton is entirely flat.
2. Put glue all over it and wrap it in Japanese paper. Make a line with your fingernail.
3. Cut off the extra paper and roll it on a flat surface.

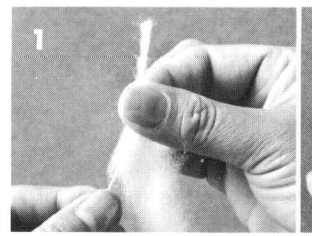

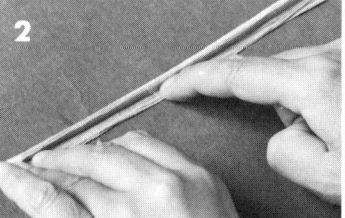

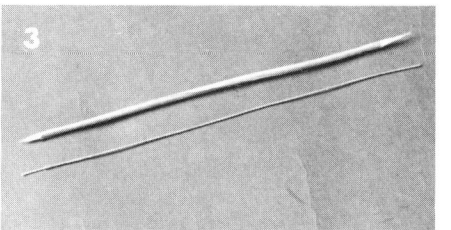

Combs ★

Two easy kinds of combs for beginners.

● The Pleated Comb
Materials:
1 piece of gathered paper 5 cm. sq. in a color you like.
1 piece of drawing paper of the same size for the lining.

How to Make It
1. Get the paper ready.
2. Glue the two pieces of paper together. Bring the two long edges together and fold to a width of 2.5 cm.
3. Fold in half widthwise and glue together.
4. Shape it by making tucks with your fingers.
5. Adjust the size and cut off the extra.

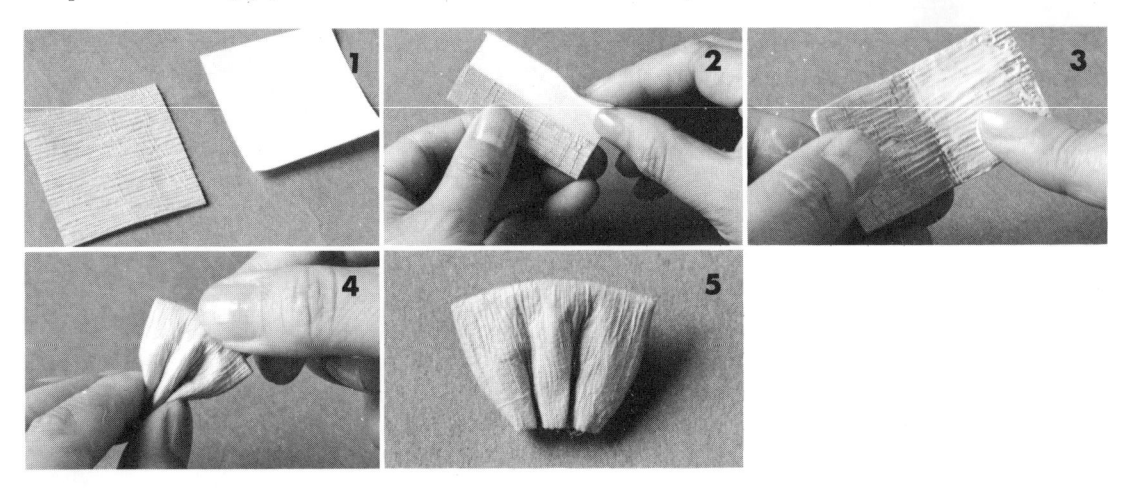

● Flat Comb
Materials:
A little gathered paper in a color you like.
Drawing paper of the same size for the lining.
Decorative string the same color as the comb.

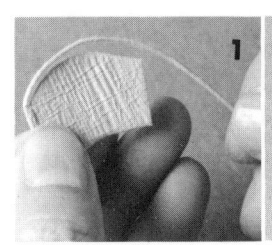

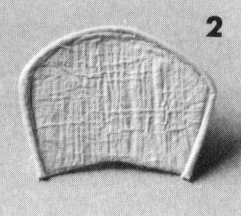

How to Make It
First, cut the paper for the lining in a shape you like. Glue some gathered paper on both sides and cut in the same shape.
1. Put glue along the edges of the comb and put decorative string along it.
2. Now you can put teeth in the comb, put flowers on it, etc.

Tassels ★

Tassels are used on the ends of string, on fringed hairpins, etc. Fringed forelocks and sidelocks are made the same way. Presented are tassels on the ends of thin string.

● Type 1 (single)
Materials:
1 piece of gathered paper for two tassels (5×6 cm.)
1 thin piece of decorative string of the same color.

How to Make It
1. Put glue on the paper.
2. Fold in two lengthwise with one edge 2 mm. lower than the other and glue together.

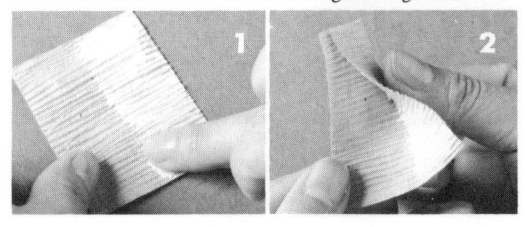

3. Make lengthwise cuts in the side with the fold, stopping 5 mm. from the top.
4. Cut it in two pieces at the center. Put glue on the 2 mm. edge.
5. Wind it around the end of a piece of thin string.
6. Roll it back and forth between your fingers. Do likewise with the other end of the string and the other tassel.

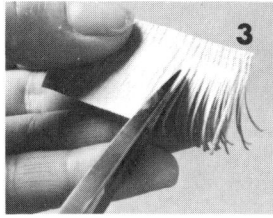

● **Type 2 (double)**
Materials:
  1 piece of gathered paper for the tassel (5× 6 cm.)
  1 thin piece of decorative string of the same color.

How to Make It
1. Put glue along the edge 5 mm. wide. Fold it in two and make it as you did the first tassel. After winding it around the end of the string, cut along the fold.
2. These are the two types of tassels. The upper one in the picture is the first type.

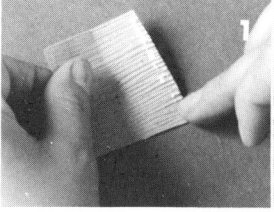

Ornamental Hairpins ★

These hairpins were first used as instruments in making chignons or putting the hair up. Later they were also used as ornament for the *Shimada* chignon, *Marumage*, etc. The basic form is flat, long and narrow.

Materials:
  1 piece of gathered colored paper for the hairpin (2×5.5 cm.)
  1 piece of drawing paper of the same size for the lining.

How to Make It
1. First, line the paper for the hairpin. Roll it lengthwise.
2. Unroll the paper and apply a little glue.
3. Roll again lengthwise from both ends. Join at the center and fix the ends with a perforator.
4. Put lots of glue at the joined edges. Shape it with your fingertips. Then crush it at the center.
5. Make it flat in the front and back.

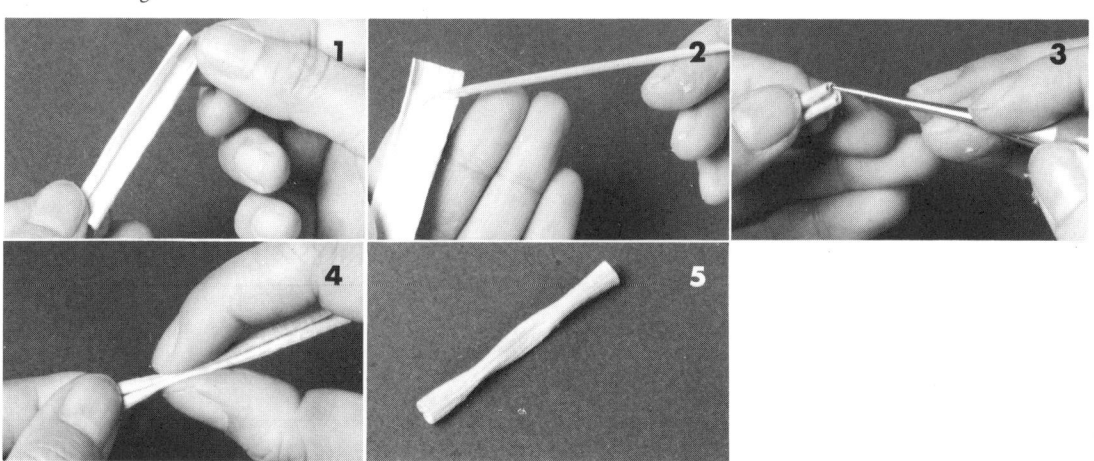

57

Flowers ★

Make cherry blossoms, chrysanthemums, peonies, etc. with the leftover paper.

Materials:
   A little gathered colored paper.
   A little drawing paper to line it.

An Easy Way to Make a Pentagon

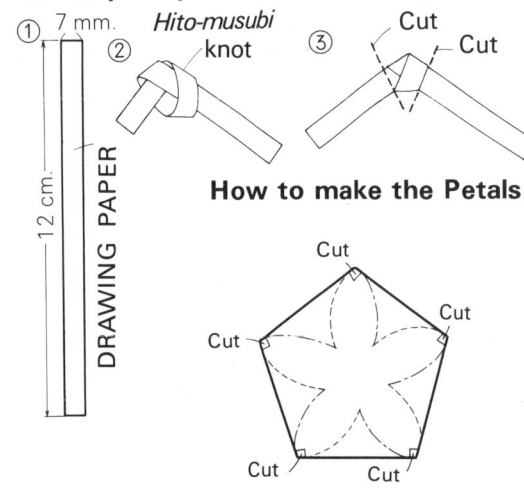

How to make the Petals

How to Make It

First, glue gathered paper to both sides of the paper for the lining. Cut in a pentagon with sides of 7 mm. (See sketch.)
1. Cut tiny triangles in the corners.
2. Use a tracer to make the rounded shape of the petals and cut. (See sketch.)
3. Place it in the palm of your hand. Using the flat end of a toothpick, push one petal at a time into your palm. This will shape it into an open flower.
4. Also push in at the center.
5. Cut some pieces of decorative string 3 mm. long. Put glue in the center of the flower and put the little pieces there with a tweezers.
6. The flowers are done.
7. Make a floral hairpin by putting some on the stick of a hairpin.

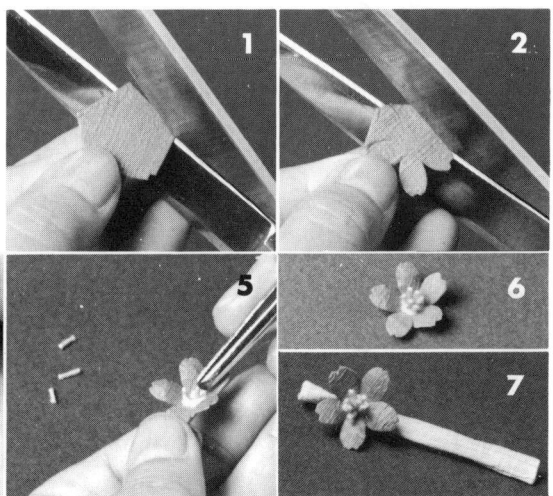

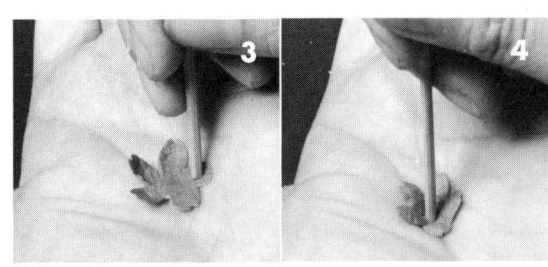

1 tassel of the second type (p. 57) of a matching color.

Fringed Hairpins ★

Make it by putting flowers and a tassel on a hairpin.

Materials:
   1 piece of gathered colored paper for the stick of the hairpin (1.6×7 cm.).
   A little paper for the lining.
   5 cherry blossoms.

How to Make the Fringed Hairpin

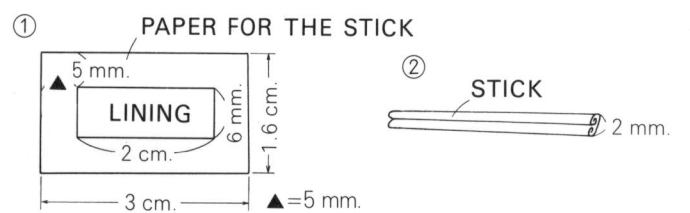

How to Make It
1. Line the paper for the hairpin.
2. Roll it lengthwise. Make it like the ornamental hairpin, but round it and do not crush it.
3. Put the flowers and a tassel on. Make the tassel with a 3 cm. sq. piece of gathered paper. Insert it under the flowers.

Bells ★

Bells are put on special dolls which are thrown in rivers, etc. for good luck. It is said that they call happiness.

Materials:
1 piece of gold gathered paper (5×10 cm.)
A little black paper.
1 cotton ball like the one used for the three year-old boy's head.
String.
A little cotton.

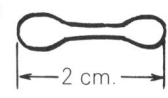

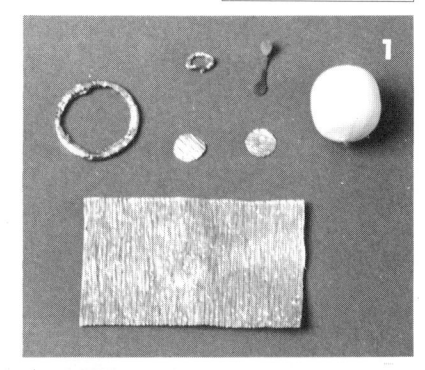

Holes
←2 cm.→
ACTUAL SIZE

How to Make It
First, make a thick string (about 3 mm. wide) by wrapping cotton in gold paper and also a thin string.

1. Get the materials ready. Make the ring around the bell by making a ring 8 cm. in diameter with thick string. Make the loop at the top of the bell by making a ring 3 cm. in diameter with thin string. Make holes with the black paper (See sketch). Make 2 pieces of paper 1 cm. in diameter for the top of the bell and 1 piece for the main part (5×9 cm.)
2. Put glue on the large piece of paper and wrap the cotton ball inside.
3. Make the top and bottom fit well.
4. Wrinkle the ends and cut off the tips. Flatten them with your fingers.
5. Mark the place for the ring with your fingernail.
6. Put glue all along the mark and put the ring on.
7. Glue the 1 cm. piece of paper on the bottom of the bell.
8. Glue the holes on over that.
9. Put the other piece of paper through the loop and glue it on the top.

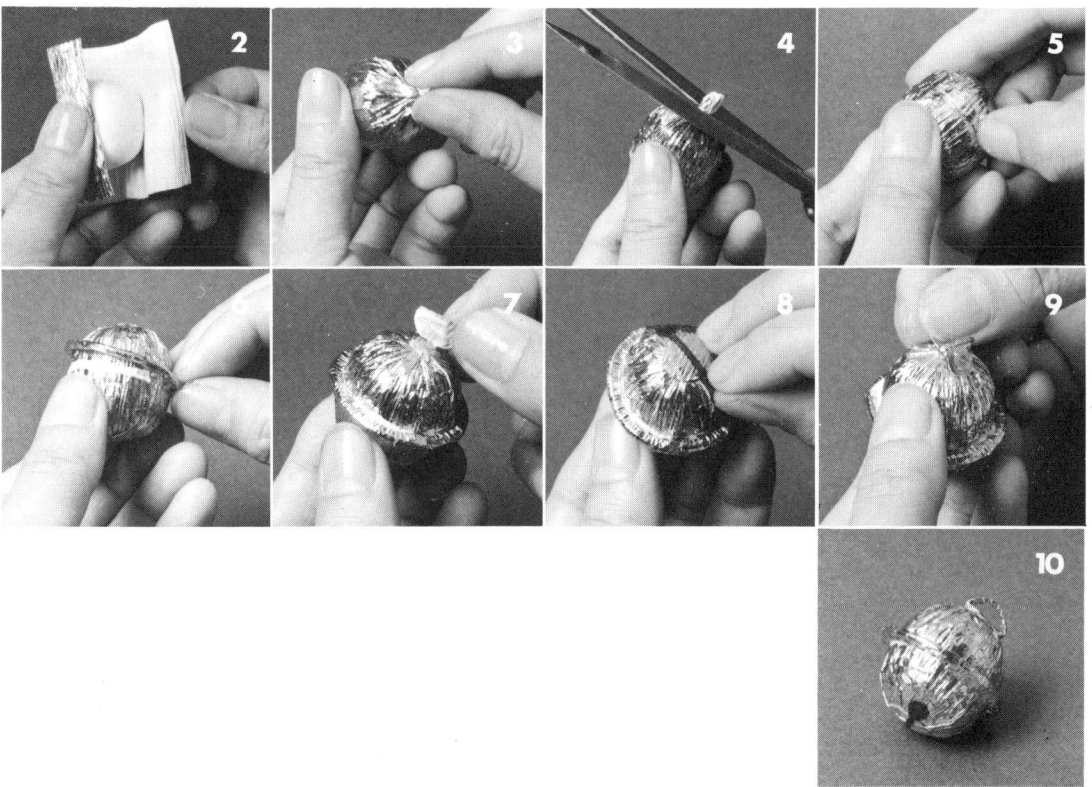

Hakama ★

The *hakama* is a pleated skirt worn by boys from the age of five. Here we layered three colors of paper for the cuffs, back opening of the long sleeve and collar. Putting the *hakama* on is complicated, so shape it before the glue dries.

Materials:
1 piece of gathered paper with a print for the *kimono* (25×21 cm.)
1 piece of gathered paper of a color that will match the *kimono* for the *hakama* (28×19 cm.)
Solid color gathered paper in 3 different colors for the cuffs, collar and sleeve opening (18×7 cm.)
1 piece of drawing paper for the lining.
A little decorative string.
A little gathered paper of the same color.
1 young man's body (put a young man's topknot on a child's body.)
A little cotton.

How to Make It
First, get the necessary materials ready. With the paper for the *hakama*, make 1 piece for the *hakama* (28×14 cm.), 1 piece (3.5×3 cm.) and 2 pieces (2×2 cm.) for the back stays, and 1 piece (25×0.5 cm.) for the hip string. Cut 2 pieces in each of the three colors for the cuffs (18×2 cm.), 2 pieces in each of the three colors for the sleeve opening (16×2 cm), and 1 piece in each color for the collar (14×3 cm.). With the drawing paper, make 3 pieces for the collar lining (13×3 cm.), 6 pieces for the cuff lining (18×1 cm.), 6 pieces for the lining of the sleeve opening (16×1 cm.), 1 piece for the lining of the back stay (3.5×3 cm.), and 1 piece for the lining of the hip string (25×0.5 cm.).

1. Line each of the three pieces of colored paper for the collar. Put them along the body and glue.
2. Fold the *kimono*. First, fold the 25 cm. long side 3 cm. to the inside and glue. Fold back to the outside 8 mm. from the fold.
3. Fit it on the body before the glue dries. Leave an area 1 cm. from the collar ridge and put glue on the rest.
4. Cut up to the armpit along the body line.
5. Make 2.5 cm. long cuts 1.5 cm. from the collar edge.
6. Cut the hemline shorter than the body in back and glue it to the legs.
7. Try the *hakama* on the body.
8. Fold in the part that extends below the body

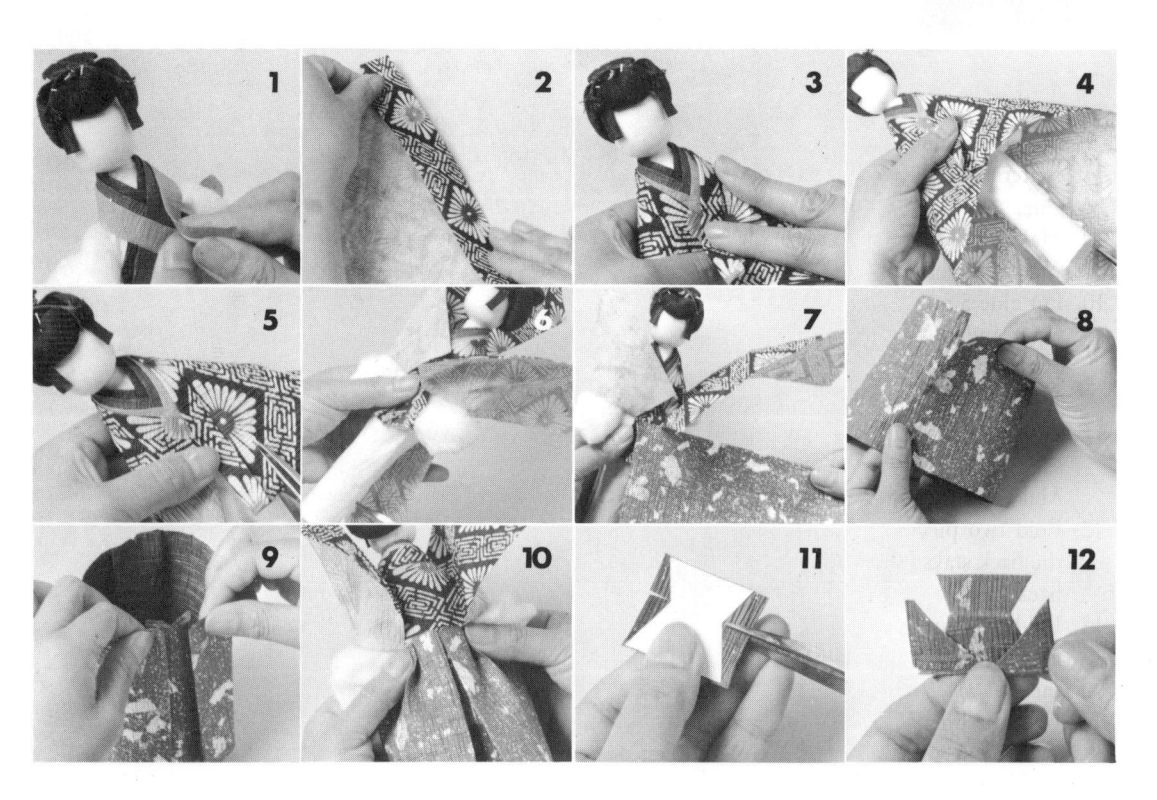

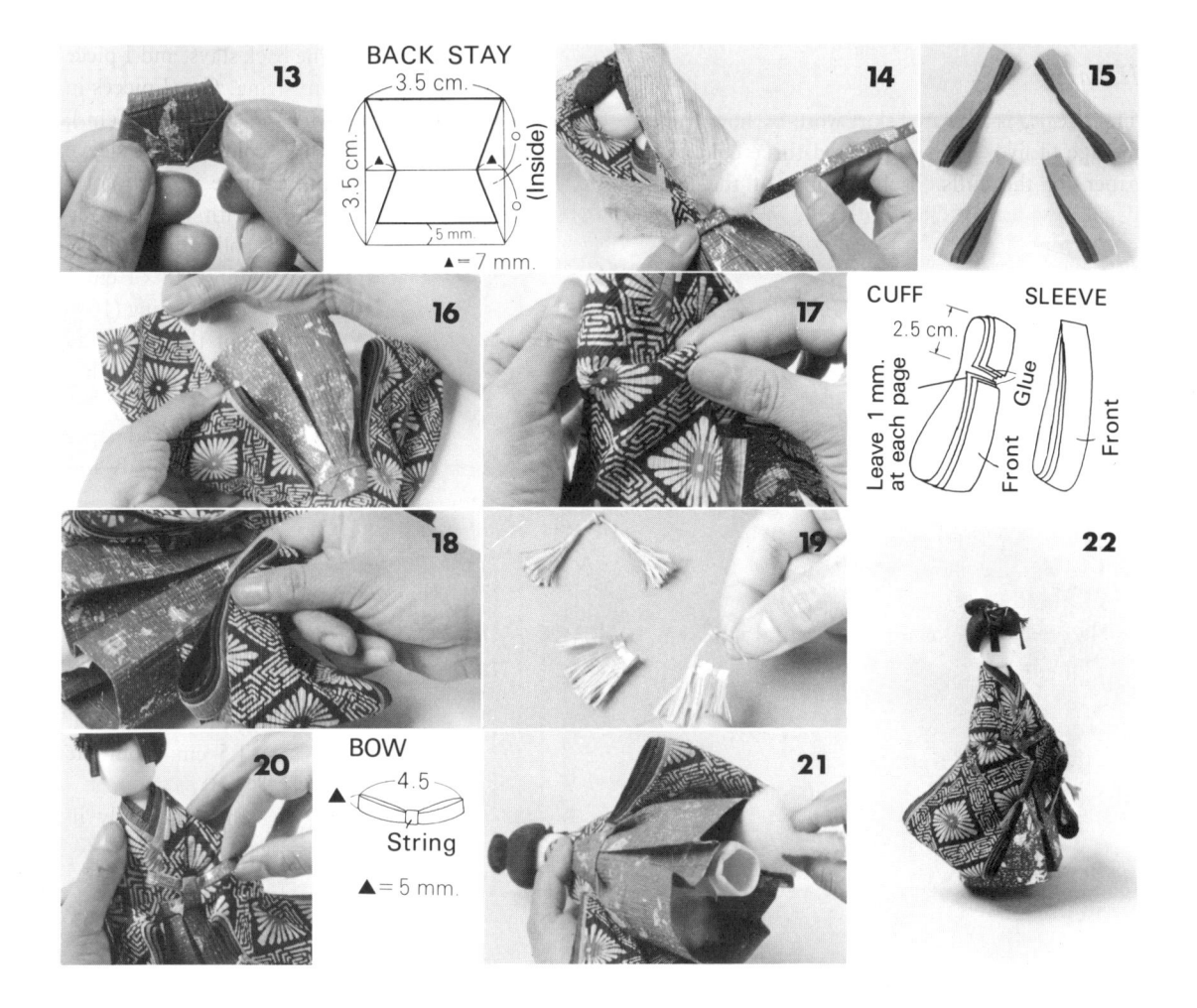

(2.5 cm.) and glue. Hold the paper so it makes a circle and mark the center front and center back. Overlap the edges 5 mm. and glue.

9. Make a 2.5 cm. box pleat at the center front and center back.
10. Put glue 5 mm. wide around the girth of the waist and put it on the body. Take in the extra by making darts 1.5 cm. to the left and right of the center.
11. Glue the pattern of drawing paper (see sketch) to the paper for the back stays. Make cuts, fold to the inside and glue.
12. Fold two pieces of the 2 cm. sq. paper for the back stays in triangles. Glue them on the back stay.
13. Fold in along the oblique lines of the stay. Fold in two and put it on the upper part of the *hakama*.
14. Fold the lined hip string in three and put it around the waist.
15. Line the cuffs and sleeve openings and put the three colors together as shown in the sketch.
16. Fold the back sleeve opening of the *kimono* in 5 mm. and glue on the three colors.
17. Shape the sleeves by putting your finger inside the cuff and folding it perpendicular to the body line.
18. Fold in the edge of the *kimono* cuffs 5 mm. and put on the three colored cuffs.
19. Tie a knot with decorative string (p. 39) and add tassels of the same color.
20. Put them on the cuffs. Make bows with the front string of the *hakama* (see sketch) and put them on. Fold them in three and shape so that the bow ends are slightly up. Glue.
21. Put cotton in under the *hakama* to make the hip line.
22. Glue down any places, such as the sleeve, that are sticking out.

Hand-lamps (p. 10) ━━━★

Many variations can be made by putting on a handle, decorating it with tassels, etc. To make it easy for beginners we will show you how to make the basic cylindrical shape.

Materials
You will make a pair of hand-lamps, but the following is for only one.
- 1 piece of drawing paper (3.5×22 cm.) for the backing.
- 1 piece of corrugated cardboard 5 cm. sq.
- 1 piece of black Japanese gathered paper (10.5×22 cm.) for the lamp stand.
- 1 piece of white Japanese gathered paper (7×18 cm.) for the lamp shade.
- A little cotton.

The completed hand-lamps will be 18 cm. high.

How to Cut It
Cut the black paper into one 3.5×22 cm. piece, one circle 5 cm. in diameter, and another 7 cm. in diameter. Using the lamp shade pattern, cut out six pieces of the white paper. Cut them so the grain is as indicated by the arrows. Cut the cardboard in a cicrle 5 cm. in diameter.

How to Make It
1. Stretch the 3.5×22 cm. piece of black paper all over and glue it to the backing. Cut a strip 5 mm. wide off the long edge of one side and set it aside. Make cuts at both ends as shown in the sketch and make it into a cylinder. The edge where glue will be applied is the black edge sticking out.
2. Open out the bottom of the black paper and glue the ends to the cardboard circle. Cut a hole in the center of the 7 cm. black circle and put the cylinder through it.
3. Put glue on the base of the stand. Put some cotton between the cardboard and the black paper.
4. Bring the black paper down to the bottom of the cylinder, so that it is flat. Glue it to the bottom. Glue the 5 cm. black circle on the underneath.
5. Curve each strip at the other end toward the center.
6. Put glue on the inside of each piece.
7. Glue one of the white pieces between two of the black strips.
8. Next, leaving every other space open, glue on two more white pieces.
9. Then glue on the remaining pieces in the spaces left open. Glue the long black strip you set aside in Step 1. along the outside rim.
10. Wind a similar strip of black paper around the base of the lamp shade and glue.

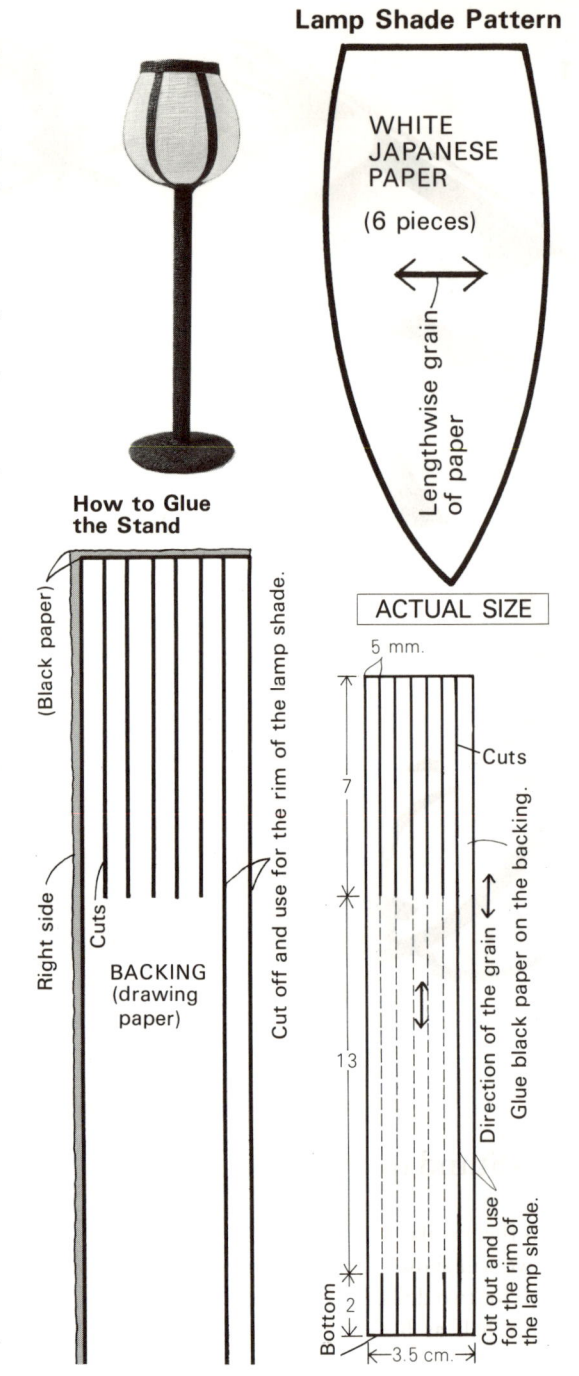

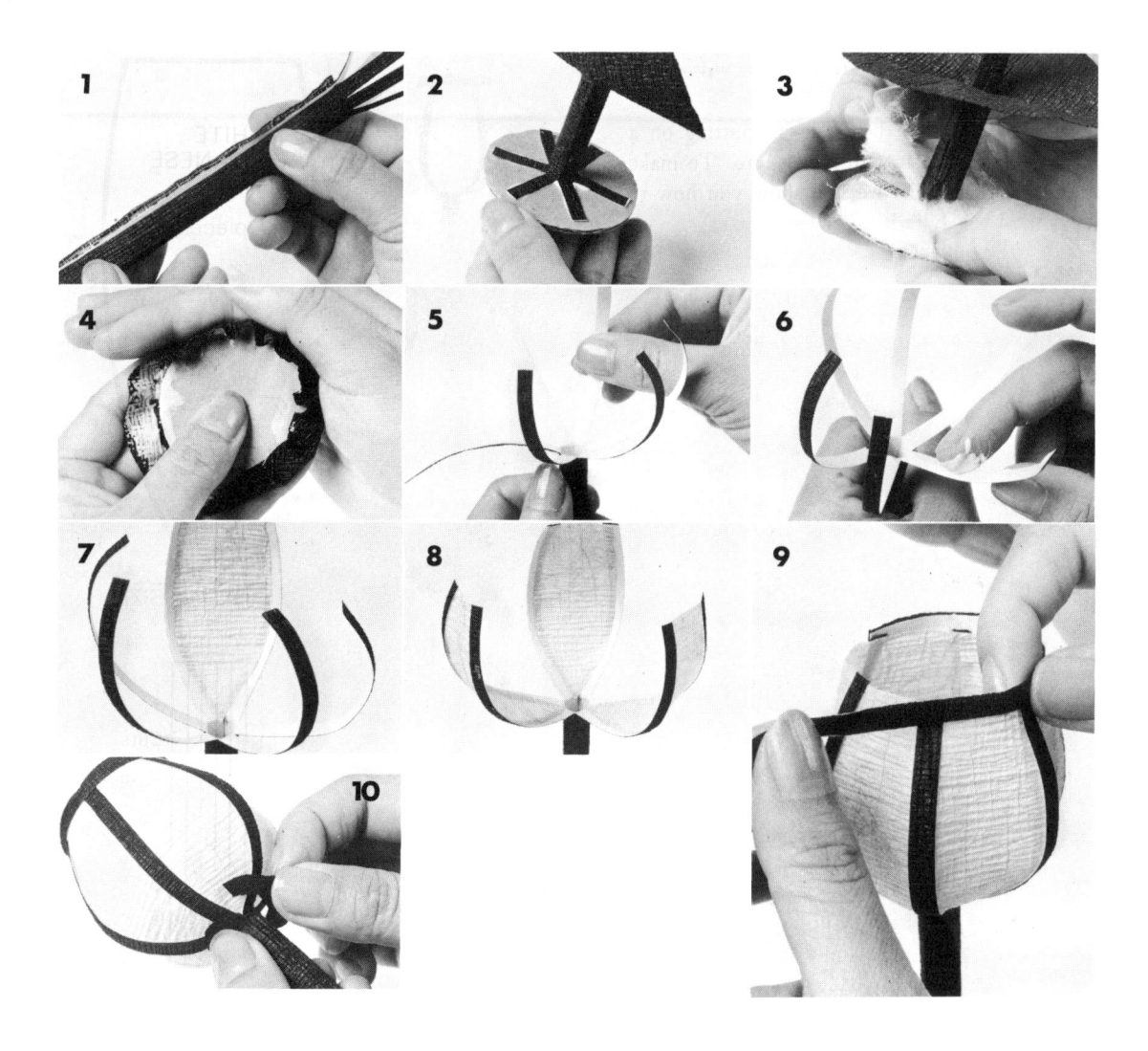

Doll-Stand (p. 10) ━━━━━━★

This is the boxlike stand that the dolls are put on. Here we will show you how to make a stand big enough for two dolls. The stands shown on p. 10 are only half as big, and the dolls are standing separately.

Materials
- 1 piece of corrugated cardboard for the backing (20×36 cm.)
- 1 piece of mustard colored Japanese gathered paper (18×38 in.)
- 1 piece of gathered paper with a print (6×38 cm.)
- 4 pieces of drawing paper for the tape (2×4 cm.)

63

The completed stand will be 16×32 cm. with a height of 2 cm.

How to Make It
1. Cut out a 2 cm. square at each corner. Fold each and 2 cm. from the edge.
2. Shape it into a box and glue the tape on at each corner.
3. Glue on the mustard colored paper, starting 1 cm. from the front edge on top.
4. Put the excess paper around the sides as shown in the picture. Glue it carefully.
5. Glue on the paper for the front of the stand, starting 2 cm. from the front edge on top. Bring the remaining paper down naturally over the edge.
6. Fold the excess paper at the corners and glue it securely.
7. Fold the remaining paper underneath and glue it.

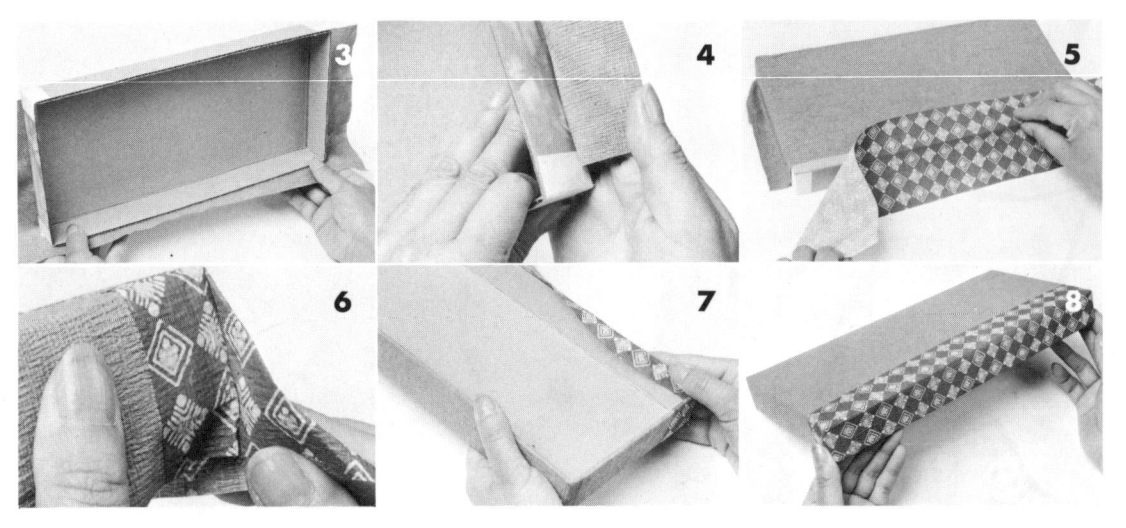

Screen (p. 10) ★

You can use just one piece of thick paper for the folding screen. We backed it and put a frame around it to make it more beautiful. Change the width, height and number of folds according to the size of the doll. Two folding screens with six make a set.

Materials
1 piece of corrugated cardboard for the backing (20×36 cm.)
1 piece of black Japanese gathered paper (24×40 cm.)
1 piece of gathered paper with a print (use one with a large print 2 cm. wide) (2×35 cm.)
1 more of the same (2×40 cm.)
1 piece of gold gathered paper (18×34 cm.)

How to Make It
1. With a paper cutter, cut five folds on both sides of the cardboard, each exactly opposite that on the other side.

Backing (cardboard)

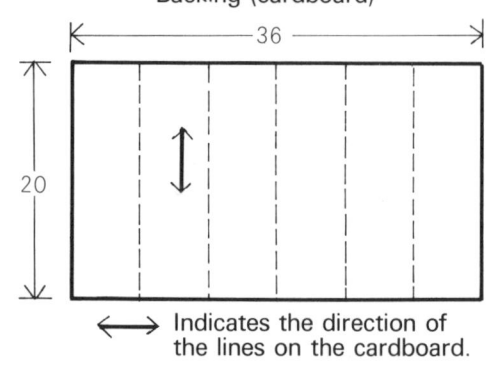

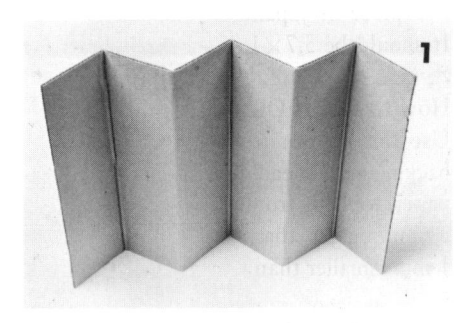

⟵⟶ Indicates the direction of the lines on the cardboard.

2. Put lots of glue on the side that will be the back and glue it to the middle of the black

paper. Hold down the lines of the folds so the shape will not be distorted.
3. First, glue the edges of the black paper around the top and bottom edges of the backing. Fold the excess at the corners. Then fold and glue the right and left edges.
4. Now you have glued on the frame.
5. Glue on the gold paper so that 1 cm. of the black frame shows at the edges.
6. Cut the paper with a print and glue it over the top edges of the gold paper.
7. Also glue it over the right and left edges so paper will not stretch. The black edges will show.

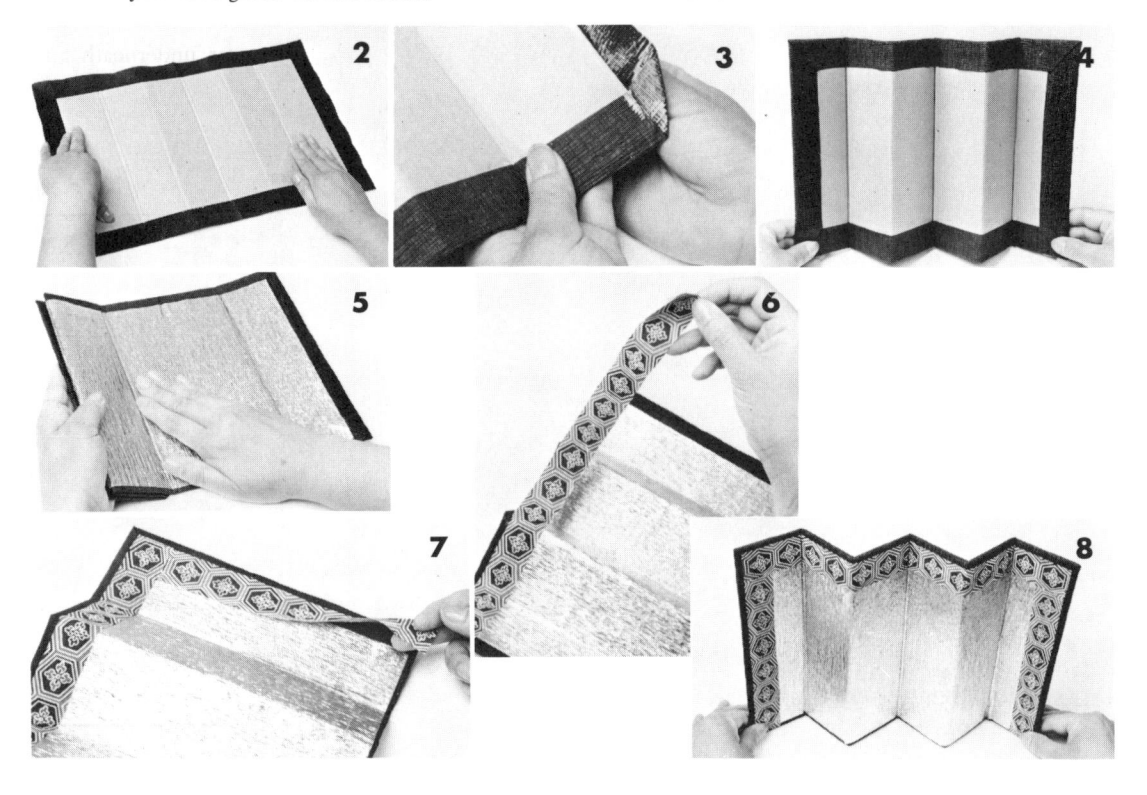

****

Scepter (p. 10) ────────★

Materials
1 piece of drawing paper for the backing (6 cm. sq.)
1 piece of Japanese paper (6 cm. sq.)
It should be 5.7×1.5 cm. when finished.

How to Cut It Out
Use the pattern to cut out the two pieces of backing (one of each grain direction). Cut out the paper for the front and back, making the front 3 mm. bigger than the bakcing and the back 1 mm. smaller than the backing.

How to Make It
Glue the two pieces of backing together. Place on top of the paper for the front. Make small cuts at the four corners, leaving a 1 mm. space from the top of the cuts to the edge of the backing. Put glue on the 3 mm. edge. Fold the edge over and glue it to the backing. Apply glue to the paper for the back and glue it on.

Two pieces of drawing paper for the backing (one of each grain direction).

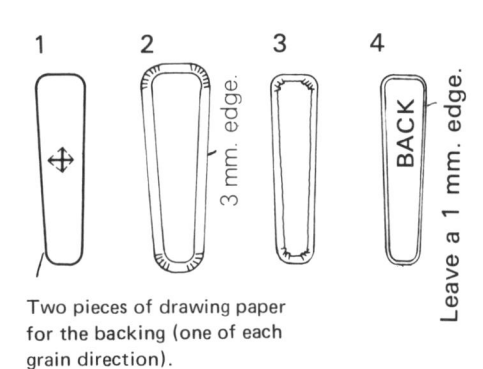

ACTUAL SIZE

65

Swords (p. 10) ━━━━★

Swords are used for the dolls for Children's Day in May or for *samurai* dolls. The size of the sword will depend on the size of the doll. Study many famous swords and make elaborate handles and sword-guards.

Materials
- 1 piece of drawing paper for the backing (3×6 cm.)
- 1 piece of gold Japanese gathered paper (3×7 cm.)
- 1 more piece (2×3 cm.), plus a little more.
- 1 piece of gathered paper with a print on a black background cut on the bias (3×21 cm.)
- 1 piece of mustard colored gathered paper (0.5×45 cm.)
- String.
- Cotton.

The completed sword should be 20 cm. from end to end.

The sword-guard is between the blade and the handle of the sword. It prevented the hand from being hit by the enemy's sword. It was a flat iron plate. The hole in the center is called the *nakago* hole. On the right is the *kogaihitsu* hole, and on the left is the *kozukahitsu* hole. Here we have used only the *nakago* hole and left out the others. Patterns and shapes changed with the times, but most usually had the circular sword-guard.

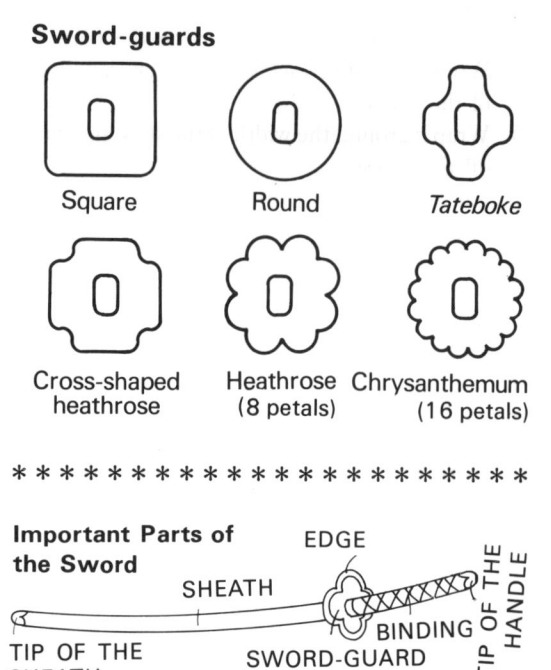

Sword-guards

- Square
- Round
- *Tateboke*
- Cross-shaped heathrose
- Heathrose (8 petals)
- Chrysanthemum (16 petals)

****

Important Parts of the Sword: EDGE, SHEATH, TIP OF THE SHEATH, SWORD-GUARD, BINDING, TIP OF THE HANDLE

How to Make It
1. Twist two pieces of string around each other.
2. The string will be the center. Cut a long, narrow piece of cotton and wind it around and down.
3. Wind around piece after piece of cotton until it is 20 cm. long and 1 cm. thick.
4. Put glue all over it. Let it dry and then adjust it.
5. Next, glue on the black piece of paper. Put lots of glue down the center lengthwise while stretching the paper. It will curve

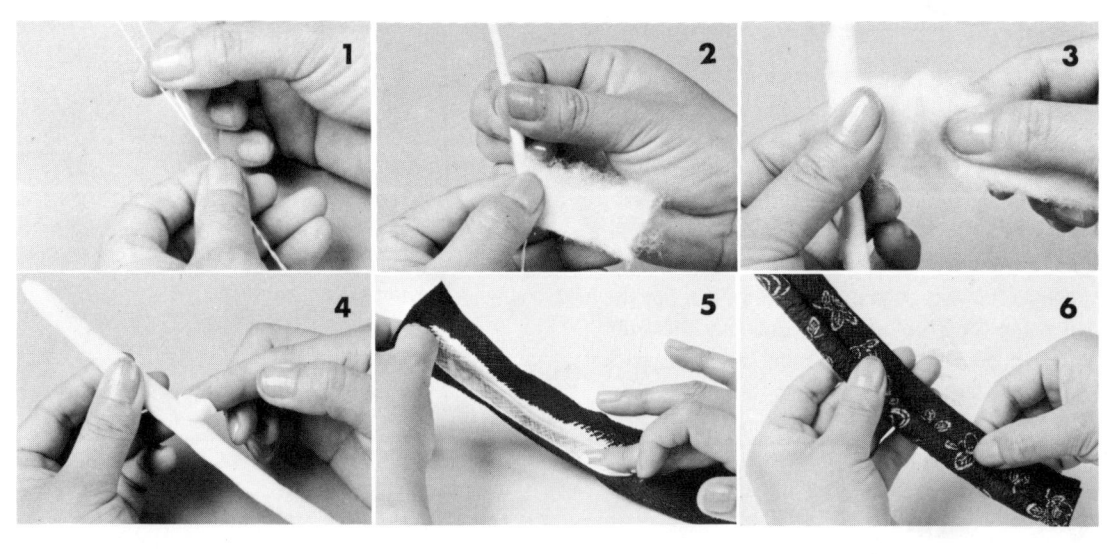

naturally because it was cut on the bias.
6. Wrap the cotton stick along the curved side of the paper.
7. Wrap it around the width of the stick and cut off the excess.
8. Cut out two pieces for the backing of the sword-guard. Make one cut along the lengthwise grain and one of the widthwise grain. Glue them together. Wind some cotton around a piece of regular string and glue it around the edge of the sword-guard.
9. Glue the gold paper on the front and back.
10. Cut the gold paper along the outer edge of the backing.
11. Fix the cut edges of the gold paper before the glue dries.
12. Put a narrow strip of gold paper around the sword at a place about ¼ the sword's length. Insert the sword through the hole in the sword-guard and bring it down to the bottom edge of the gold strip. Secure it with glue. (The hole in the center will open when the sword is put through.)
13. Wind another strip of narrow gold paper around the sword underneath the sword-guard.
14. Cut some gold paper the same width as the sword and put on the tips of the scabbard and handle.
15. Wind a 5 mm. wide strip of mustard colored paper around and down the handle. Make it cross over many times and glue the end.

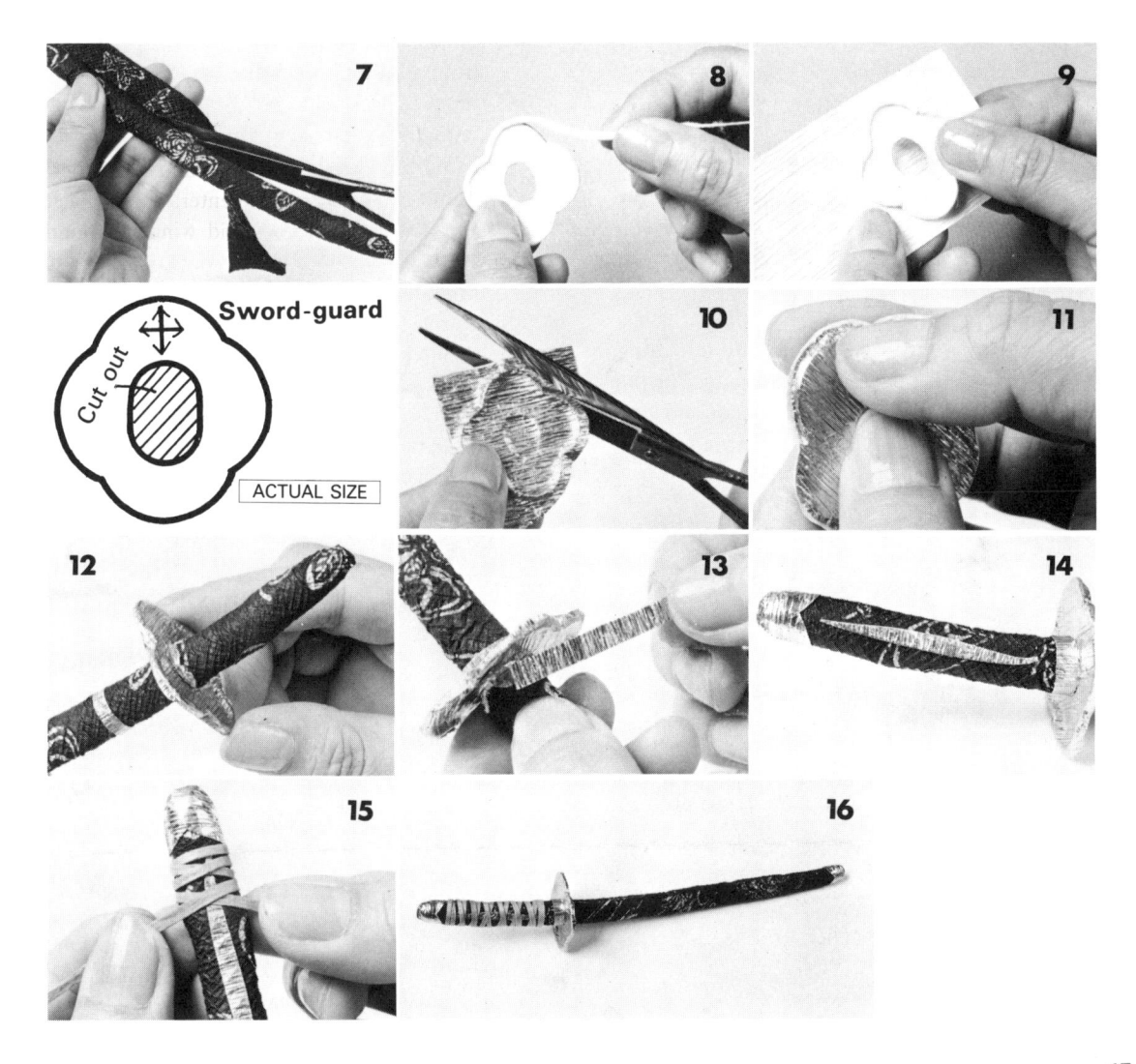

Sword-guard

Cut out

ACTUAL SIZE

67

Dwarf's Bowl (p. 11) ★

The bowl used as a dwarf's boat was that used in the kitchen. It was probably made of lacquerware with red inside. Choose some paper that is black and has a gold print for the outsied.

Materials
1 piece of drawing paper for the backing (15 cm. sq.)
1 piece of red Japanese gathered paper for the inside (13×17 cm.)
1 piece of black gathered paper with a gold print for the outside (16.5×21 cm.)
String.
Cotton.

The completed bowl should be 4 cm. high with a rim circumference of 9 cm.

Pattern for the bottom and sides of the bowl. (Use drawing paper.)

How to Make It (See sketch.)
1. Using the pattern for reference, cut out the backing for the sides and bottom of the bowl. Glue the paper for the inside of the bowl to the backing without cutting it.
2. Make cuts as shown on p. 69. Make it in the shape of a bowl. Cover the bottom backing with the same paper and glue it on. Put the bottom in the bowl from the inside and glue it. Fix the shape of the bowl with your fingertips before the glue dries.

Pattern for the Bottom and Sides of the Bowl (use drawing paper)

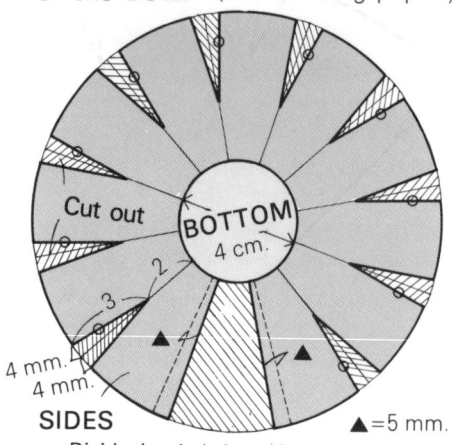

Divide the circle into 12 parts and cut out the parts.
○ marks the places you will make the cuts.

3. Wind some cotton around two pieces of string until they are 3 mm. wide.
4. Cut the black and gold paper as shown in ②. Cut four. Put some glue on and put them flat on the sides of the bowl. Also glue the 5 mm. wide edge to the bottom.
   Glue the string around the inside edge of the rim. Roll the black paper over inside to cover the string and glue.
5. Glue a piece of cotton covered string to the bottom of a 1×14 cm. piece of drawing paper. Glue on a 2.6×14 cm. piece of black paper as shown in ④. and glue it to the bottom of the bowl.
6. Glue the black circle on the bottom.

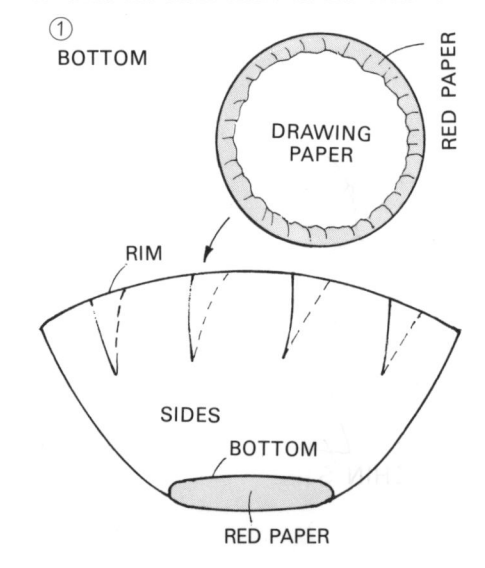

68

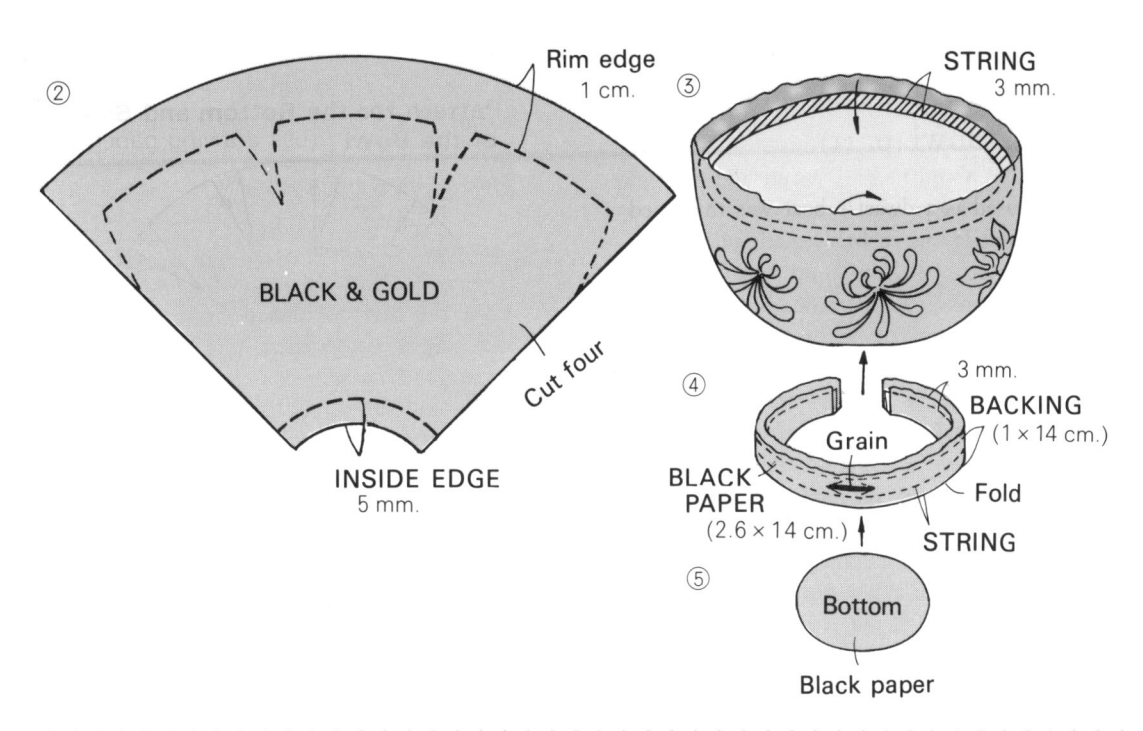

Face-guard (p. 10) ★

Materials
- 2 pieces of Japanese paper for the inside and outside (3.5 × 18.5 cm.)
- A little of the same for the chin strap.
- 1 piece of thick paper for the backing (3.5 × 18.5 cm.)
- A little of the same for the chin strap.
- 2 pieces of thick string.

How to Make It
Leave a 5 mm. edge for gluing on the Japanese paper for the inside. Apply glue and glue it to the thick paper. Glue the string on as shown in the sketch. Put on the chin strap (made by wrapping the thick paper in the Japanese paper). Glue on the paper for the outside.

Hair Ornaments ━━━━━━★

Japan has an abundance of beautiful hairstyles and ornaments. For example, there is the cute chignon band of the *Momoware* chignon made of red dappled cloth, the coral hairpin of the *Shimada* chignon, the boxwood comb of the round chignon, etc. The history of and changes in the chignons, the origin of the hairpins, etc. are just some of the deeply interesting things there are to talk about.

Long ago in the *Edo* Period the clothes and *Shimada* for the *samurai* and the merchants were decided, but with dolls, this is not necessary. Just think up any style you like.

Now, to give you a few hints for when you actually make the doll, we will show you some hairstyles and becoming ornaments.

1. *Hyogo* chignon
This is also called the *Tachihyogo* chignon and is often seen on courtesans. It is composed of a chignon which has the forelock pulled far back. It is held down with a comb, stabilized with a broad hairpin and balanced with front, back and flat hairpins. It is easy to put together if you make it into an inverted triangle and hold it down with combs and hairpins.

2. Round chignon
This is the well known chignon of the married woman. It is tied securely with wide string because the base of the chignon is high. A chignon band can also be used. The forelock can be changed by putting in floral hairpins, round ones, etc. Change the size of the back-hair, sidelocks and chignon according to the *kimono* you put on the doll.

3. *Shimada* chignon
This is one of the *Shimada* chignons. It differs from the *Hyogo* chignon in that it curves naturally from the base and is balanced with a *takenaga*. A hairpin is used to hold down the comb and keep the chignon from slipping. Curl and shape the ends of the *takenaga* before the glue dries.

4. *Kamuro* chignon
This was a chignon used during the late *Edo* Period by the young helpers of courtesans. This is a special hairstyle in which more emphasis is put on the ornaments than on the hairstyle. The center ornament is made of three cotton-filled bows tied together. It covers the base of the chignon. Tie the three bows together so they all look like butterfly wings.

5. *Yuiwata* chignon
This is a style in which all the hair is brought up in one place. The sidelocks, back hair and chignon are all big. It can be a girl or older woman's style according to what color of chignon band is used.

6. Modified *Shimada* chignon
The shape of this style is not excatly decided. We tried it with a short fringed front hairpin, a long fringed back hairpin and a chignon hairpin.

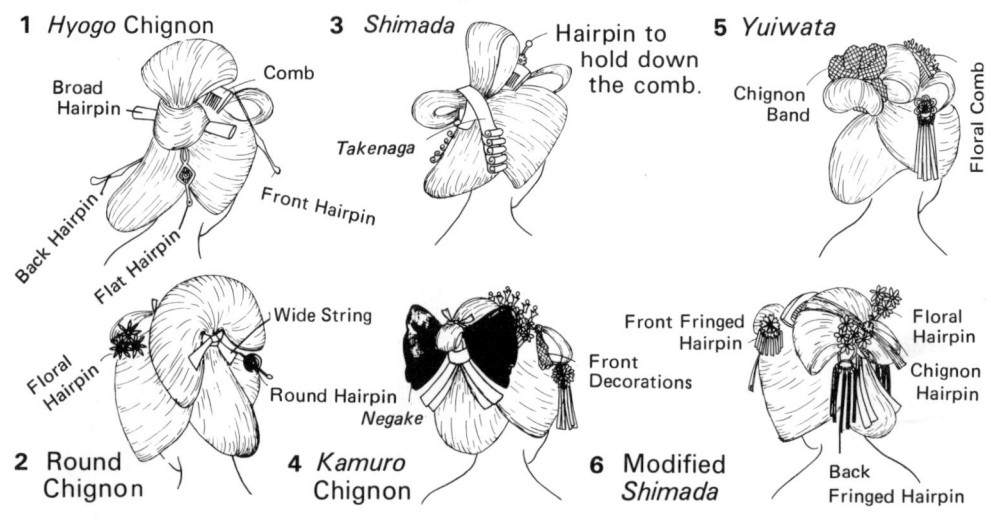

Flat Hairpin

Materials
1 piece of drawing paper for the backing (1×7 cm.)
1 piece of Japanese gathered paper (2×7 cm.)
String.
Cotton.

Upper part
Lower part
ACTUAL SIZE

How to Make It
1. Put the pattern for the hairpin on the paper for the backing.
2. Shape a 2 mm. thick piece of string with cotton wound around it according to the pattern. Make the top hole by using a toothpick.
3. Make the middle hole with a 8 mm. gathering stick.
4. Glue the shaped string on the pattern.
5. Cut the paper in the same shape as the string.
6. Fold the Japanese paper in two lengthwise. Put glue all over the inside. Put the string from Step 5 inside and glue, pressing it together with your palms.
7. To make the string inside stand out, press down on it with the gathering stick. Cut it the same shape as the string.

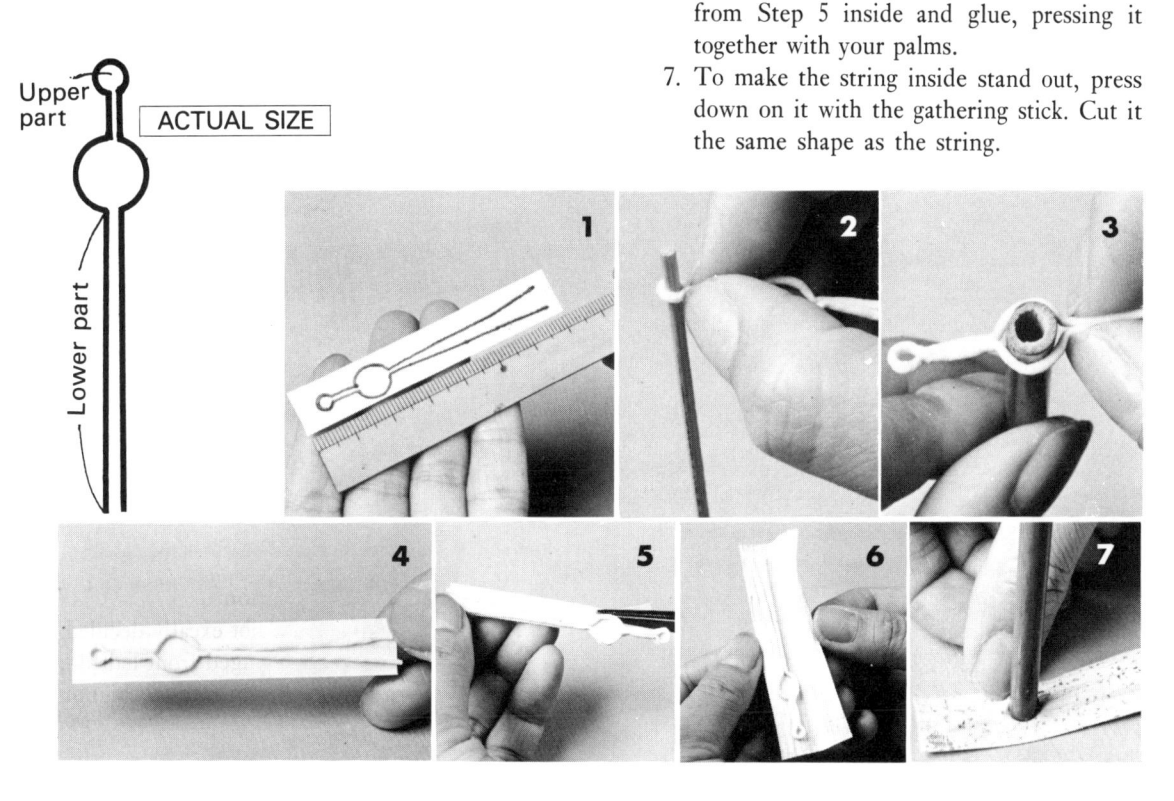

Round Hairpin

This is made by putting a ball between the upper and lower parts.

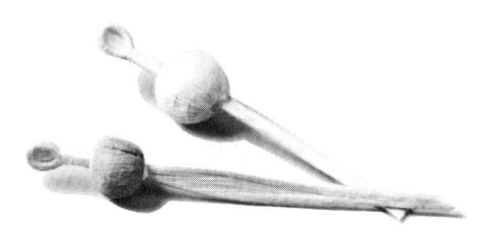

Materials
1 piece of Japanese gathered paper (2 cm. sq.)
Cotton.
1 flat hairpin made according to the pattern. The completed hairpin should be about 7 cm. long.

ACTUAL SIZE

71

How to Make It
1. Cut the Japanese paper in a circle about 2 cm. in diameter and put lots of glue on it.
2. Make a ball with the cotton and wrap it in the paper from Step 1. You can use a small stick as an axis in making the ball.
3. Cut the upper and lower parts of the hairpin apart. Choose a color of paper for the ball that will go with that of the hairpin.
4. Glue the ball between the upper and lower parts.

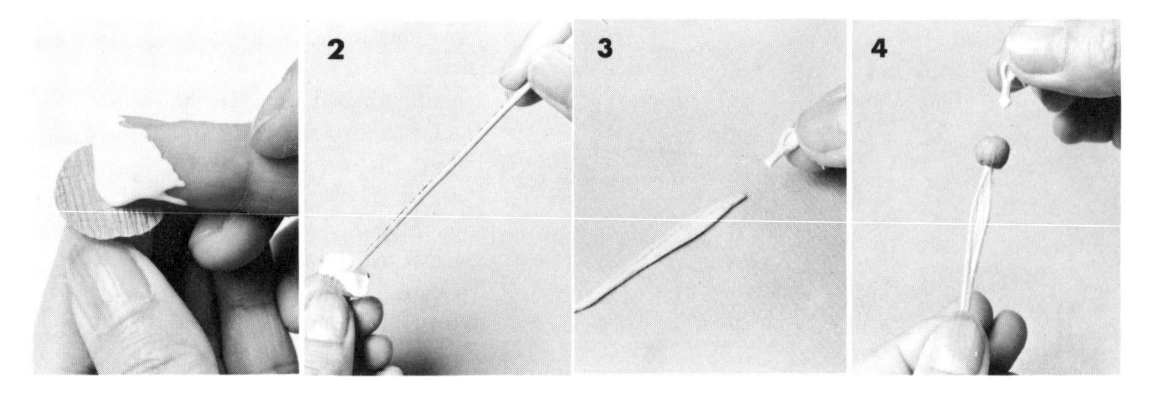

Comb and Broad Hairpin 1

These are flat and are made with paper that has a floral print. You can think up many ways to arrange the floral print.

Materials
1 piece of drawing paper for the backing (8 × 9 cm.)
1 piece of green Japanese gathered paper with a floral print for the front and back of the comb and hairpin.
String.

How to Cut It Out
Put the pattern against the paper. Pay attention to the grain direction when cutting. Make the Japanese paper for the back of the comb 3 mm. bigger than the pattern. Cut the paper for the front the same size as the pattern. Cut out two pieces with the floral print (2.5 × 2.7 cm.). Cut one plain piece for the center (2.5 × 4 cm.). Decide the exact position of the print in the front.

How to Make It (See sketch)

Do as shown in Step ①. Next, glue the paper on the back of the backing. Cut small pieces of string and glue them on for the teeth. Then glue the paper for the front, starting at the top.

Wind A and B around the ends of the backing and glue. Do the same with the plain piece in the center and glue.

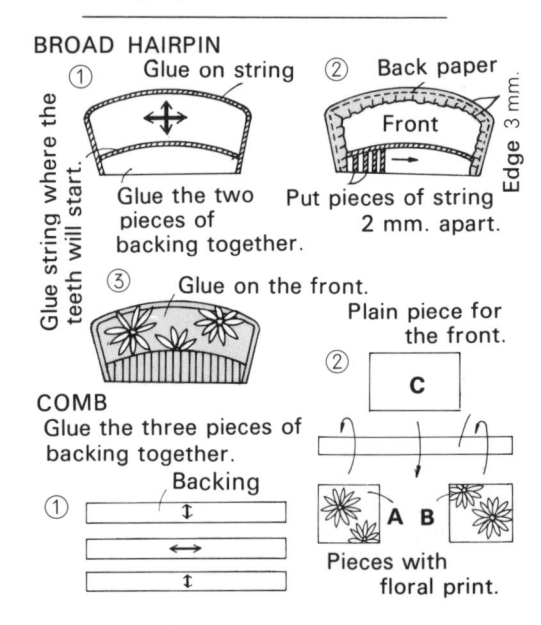

BROAD HAIRPIN
① Glue on string
Glue string where the teeth will start.
Glue the two pieces of backing together.
② Back paper
Front
Edge 3 mm.
Put pieces of string 2 mm. apart.
③ Glue on the front.
Plain piece for the front.
② C

COMB
Glue the three pieces of backing together.
① Backing
A B
Pieces with floral print.

72

Pattern for the Backing

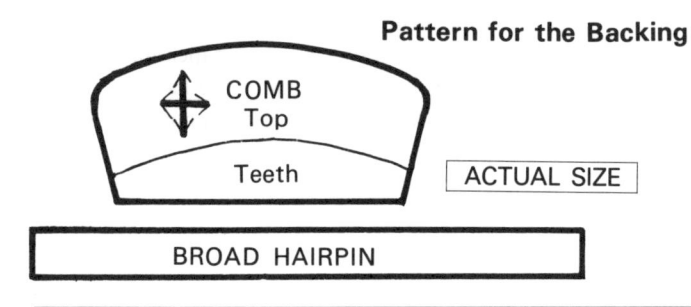

ACTUAL SIZE

COMB Top / Teeth

BROAD HAIRPIN

Cut two for the comb (one of each grain direction). Cut three for the hairpin (two lengthwise grain one widthwise grain or vice versa).

Comb and Broad Hairpin 2

The hairpin is round and the comb is shaped like a half moon. It is a basic style combined with the one on the previous page.

Materials
1 piece of drawing paper for the backing (6×4 cm.)
1 piece of brown Japanese gathered paper with a floral print for the front and back.
String.
Cotton.

How to Cut It Out
Put the pattern for the comb on the backing and cut out two (one of each grain). Make the piece of brown paper for the front 3 mm. bigger than the backing. Cut the one for the back the same size as the backing. The paper for the hairpin will be explained in the next part.

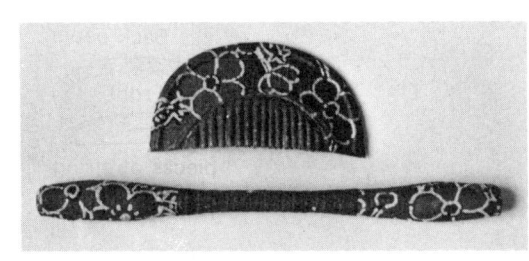

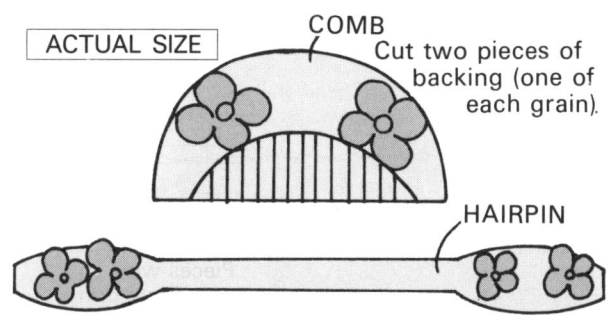

ACTUAL SIZE

COMB — Cut two pieces of backing (one of each grain).

HAIRPIN

How to Make It (See sketch)
Comb
Glue the two pieces of backing together. Glue on the string. Glue string on where the teeth start and also as on p. 72. Next, separate the paper for the front into the upper part (print) and teeth (plain). Glue them on the backing. Put the outer edges over the back. Glue the paper for the back on.

Hairpin
Wind cotton around some string until it is about the size of the pattern. Cut the brown paper into a plain piece for the center and floral pieces for the ends.
Glue them on.

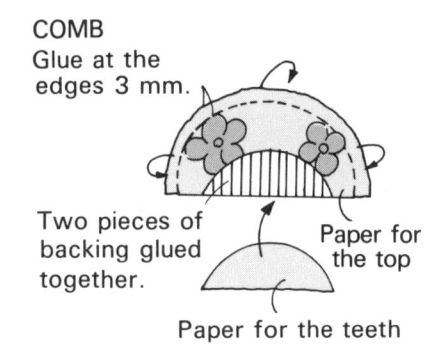

COMB
Glue at the edges 3 mm.

Two pieces of backing glued together.

Paper for the top

Paper for the teeth

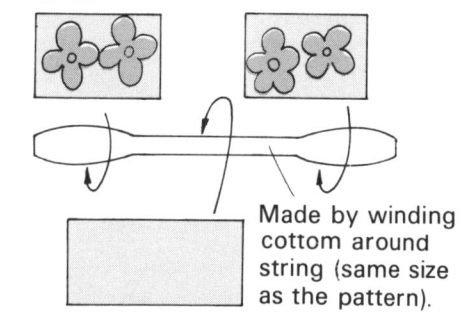

HAIRPIN

Made by winding cottom around string (same size as the pattern).

Comb and Broad Hairpin 3

Use paper that has a Japanese pine bough print for the comb. Plum blossoms and bamboo leaves are used for the ends of the hairpin. These are worn for some celebration or happy event.

Materials
1 piece of drawing paper for the backing (4×6 cm.)
1 piece of white Japanese gathered paper which has a print containing pine boughs, plum blossoms and bamboo leaves.
A little paper for the back.

How to Make It (See sketch)
Comb
See p. 72.

Hairpin
Make the body of the hairpin. Cut out the plum blossoms and bamboo leaves out. Make backing for each, glue them to the backing and glue them on the ends of the hairpin. This kind of hairpin is easier to insert in the hairdo than the flat kind.

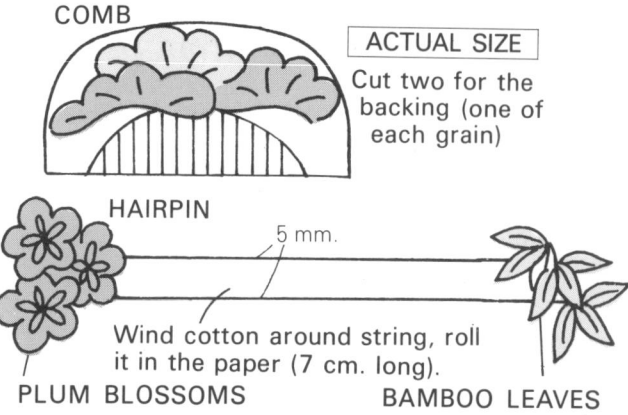

COMB

ACTUAL SIZE
Cut two for the backing (one of each grain)

HAIRPIN
5 mm.
Wind cotton around string, roll it in the paper (7 cm. long).
PLUM BLOSSOMS   BAMBOO LEAVES

Comb and Broad Hairpin 4

These are made with an openwork design. Both ends of the hairpin have open spaces.

Materials
1 piece of drawing paper for the backing (4× 6.5 cm.)
1 piece of Japanese gathered paper with a wavelike print.
String.
Cotton.
4 pieces of decorative string covered with the same paper.

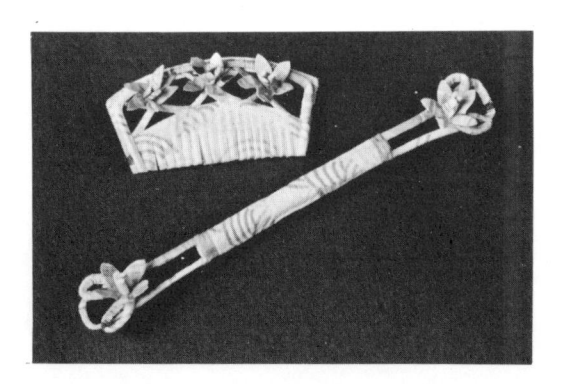

How to Make It (See sketch)
Comb
Cut out two pieces of backing, one in each grain direction, and glue them together. Put regular string around the outside as shown in ①. Next, cut the paper for the back 3 mm. bigger than the backing. Glue it on and cut a hole in the upper part as shown in ②. Make a zigzag pattern over the hole with two pieces of decorative string. Glue on the paper for the teeth and the back paper to hold the string down as shown in ③. Do as shown in ④.

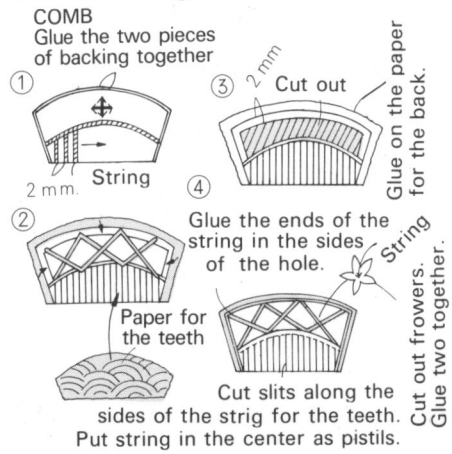

COMB
① Glue the two pieces of backing together
2 mm. String
③ Cut out 2 mm
Glue on the paper for the back.
② Paper for the teeth
④ Glue the ends of the string in the sides of the hole.
String
Cut out frowers. Glue two together.
Cut slits along the sides of the strig for the teeth. Put string in the center as pistils.

Comb Backing (cut two)

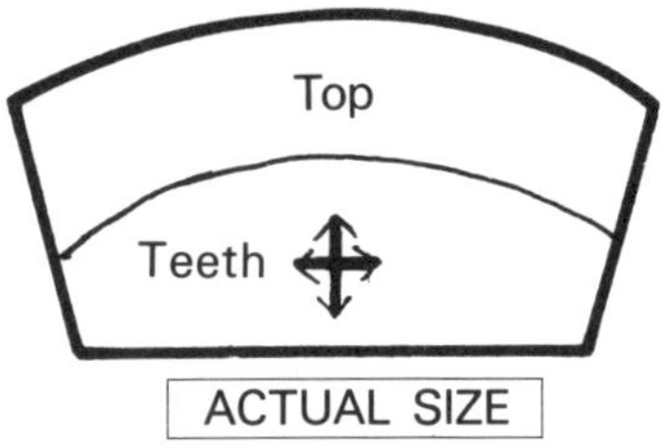

Top
Teeth

ACTUAL SIZE

HAIRPIN
Make the body by winding cotton aroung regular string. Roll it in the paper. Make the outer loops with decorative string and insert it in the main body.

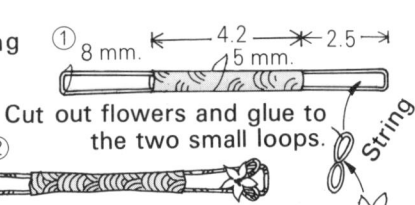

① 8 mm. ← 4.2 → ← 2.5 →
5 mm.

② Cut out flowers and glue to the two small loops.

String

★Cover the decorative string with same paper used for the main body.

Comb and Fringed Hairpin with Plum Blossoms

The comb is made in relief and plum blossoms are added. The hairpin has short fringe.

Materials

1 piece of drawing paper for the backing (3.5 × 6 cm.)
1 piece of parrot green Japanese gathered paper for the front and back of the comb (4.5 × 6 cm.)
A little light yellow gathered paper for the stick and ball of the hairpin.
1 piece of silver gathered paper for the fringe (about 4 cm. sq.)
A little pink gathered paper for the flowers.
String.
Cotton.
Yellow decorative string.

How to Make It (See sketch)
Hairpin
Make a ball and decorative string with the light yellow paper. Glue the ball on the end of the stick. Put glue on the ball and put on the plum blossoms (See sketch ②).

1. Wrap a 0.8 cm. cotton ball in the yellow paper. Wind yellow paper around a piece of string.
2. Glue two pieces of pink paper together and cut out the flowers.
3. Fringe: Fold in two. Make holes at the top.
4. Loops: Fold the silver paper in three. Put it through the holes to make the loops. Use two loops for each hold.
5. Make the big loop as in Step 4. Glue it to the main body.

HAIRPIN
① Wrap a 8mm. cotton ball in the yellow paper.
Wind yellow paper around a piece of string.
② PLUM BLOSSOMS
Glue two pieces of pink paper together and cut out the flowers.

③ LOOPS
4
1.2
PAPER SILVER
FRINGE
Fold in two. Make holes at the top.

ACTUAL SIZE

④ LOOPS
Fold the silver paper in three. Put it through the holes to make the loops. Use two loops for each hole.

⑤ Make the big loop as in Step 4. Glue it to the main body.

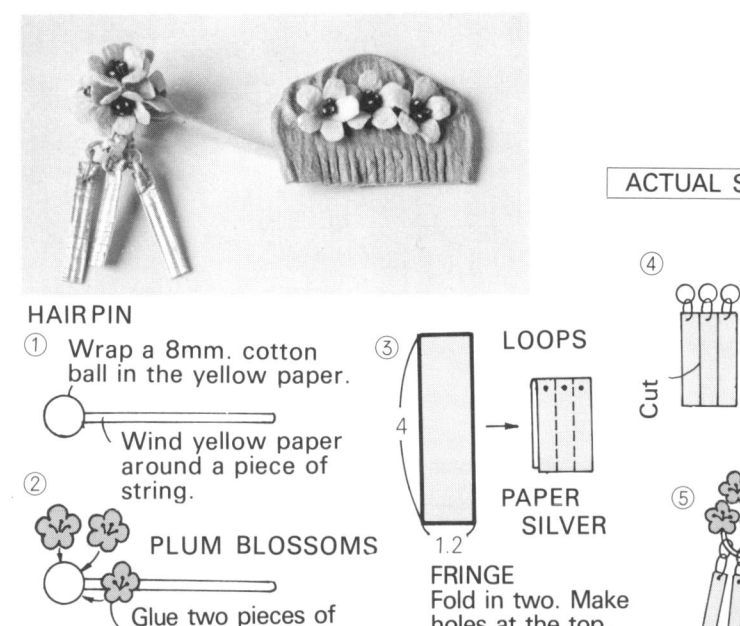

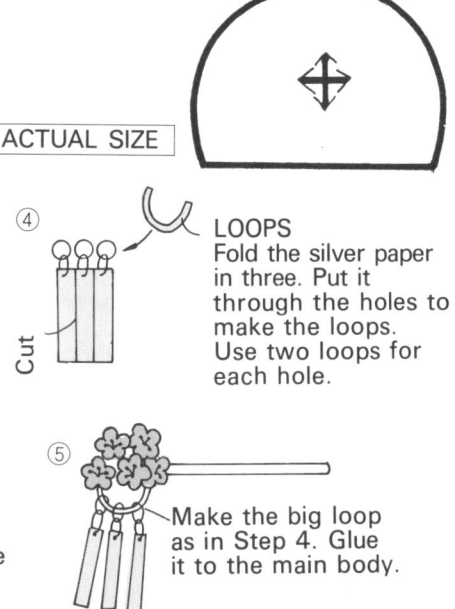

Comb

Glue the two pieces of backing together. Glue on 0.7 cm. long pieces of string for the teeth. Next, glue string on the upper part in spirals. Cut the paper for the front of the comb 3 mm. bigger than the backing. Glue it on, gluing the edge over the back. Cut the paper for the back the same size as the backing. Glue it on flat. Make flowers with the pink paper. Glue three little pieces of decorative string in the center of the flowers. Glue them on the comb as shown in ③.

Pattern for the Comb Backing

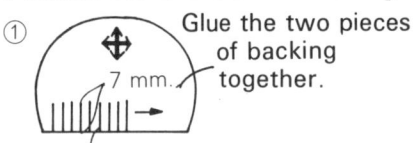

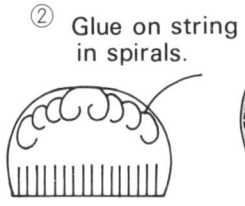

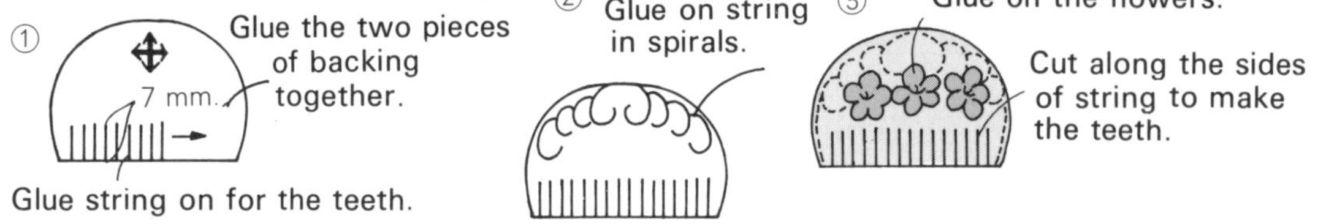

① Glue the two pieces of backing together. 7 mm. Glue string on for the teeth.

② Glue on string in spirals.

③ Glue on the flowers. Cut along the sides of string to make the teeth.

Broad and Narrow Floral Hairpins

These are very simple to make. Just put clusters of flowers near both ends. Use two kinds of Japanese paper for the flowers and leaves of the narrow hairpin.

Floral decoration 1: Just put flowers and leaves on a stem.

Floral decoration 2: Put two flowers together, one on top of the other, and you have an eight-petaled flower.

Floral decoration 3: Put decorative string along the outer edge of the petals.

Floral decoration 4: Make the center of the flower by wrapping a cotton ball in paper.

Floral decoration 5: Make lots of cuts in some Japanese paper to make the center look like fringe.

Broad Floral Hairpin: Put the flowers on loops and put the end of a flat hairpin through it. This hairpin is easy to put on or take off.

Dolls with Arms and Legs ═══★

After you have made some dolls, you will want to make many other kinds. Recently there have been many requests for dolls with arms and legs. In response to this demand we will show you how to make them for your reference. You can also use the dwarf on p. 10 or the *samurai* on p. 11 as example.

How to Make It
Arms and Hands
1. Tear a 5 mm. thick piece of cotton into ten long pieces. These will be the fingers.
2. Wind one of the ten pieces around a piece of string and make it look like a finger. Do likewise with all ten pieces.
3. Take five of them and arrange them in the shape of a hand.
4. First, stabilize the three middle fingers by winding a piece of cotton around them.
5. Next, add the little finger and thumb and wrap the cotton around again.
6. Now the left hand is done.
7. Next, wind piece after piece of cotton around to get the shape of the arm.
8. The right hand will have a battle-ax. The left hand will hold a bird, so bend it at the elbow and wind on more cotton.

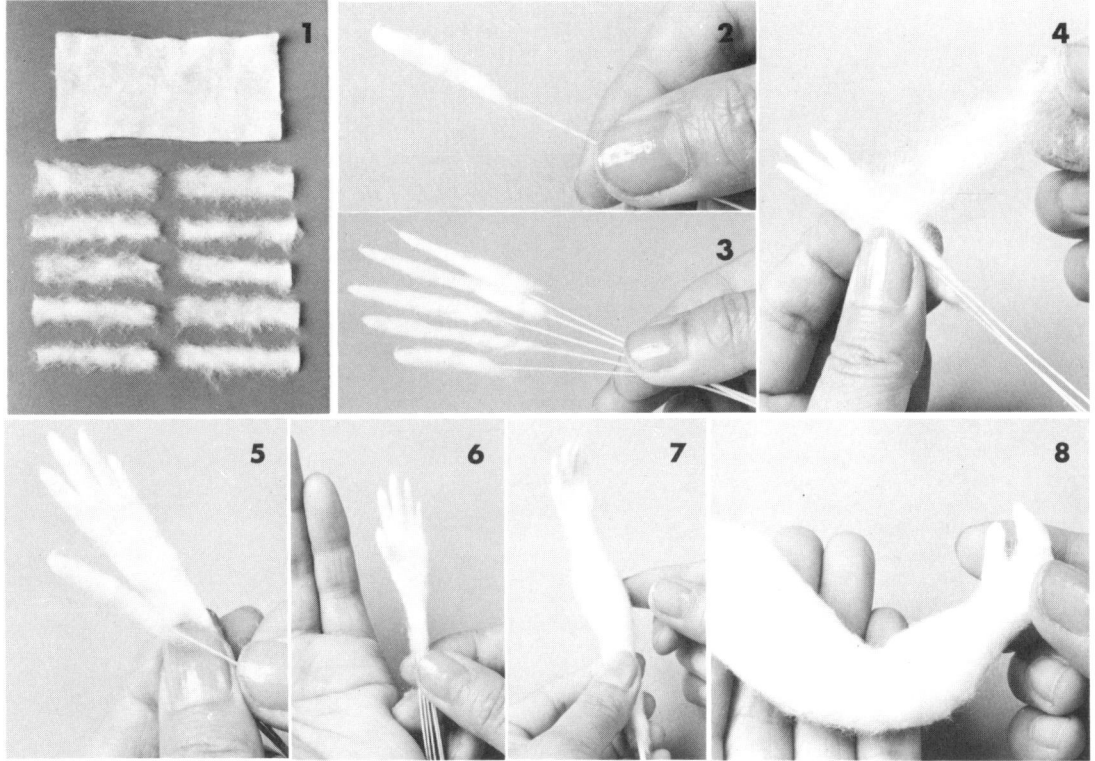

Legs
1. Make the toes the same way as the fingers. Arrange five of them in the shape of a foot and wind piece after piece of cotton around.
2. Tie string around the cotton to make the heel.
3. Bring the ends of the string up with the string from the toes.
4. Wind around more cotton.
5. Put on many pieces where the calves and thighs will be.

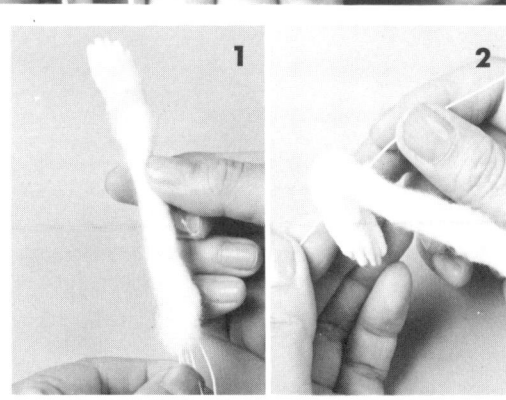

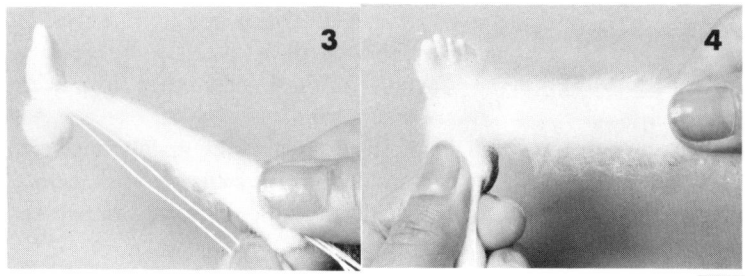

How to Put It Together
1. Make the torso about the same size as the child's torso shown on p. 21. Make the torso short because legs will be put on.
2. Glue on the arms and legs.

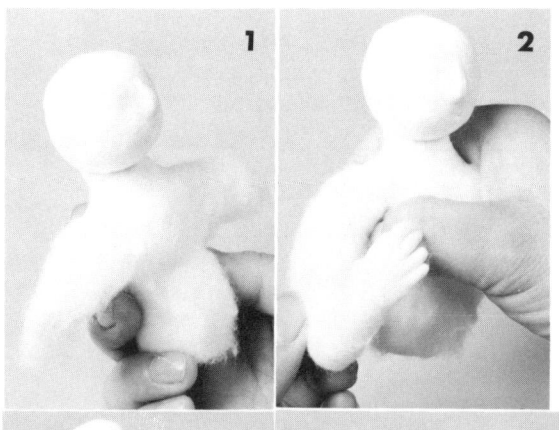

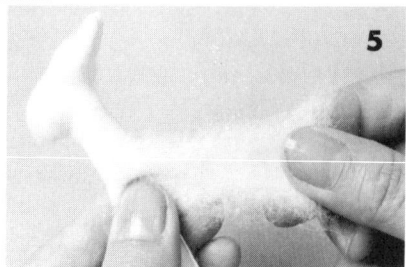

3. Cut off the excess cotton at the joint of the legs to make them easier to put on and glue.
4. Tie string around to make sure the legs will not fall off the torso.
5. Wind more cotton around it and make the hips.

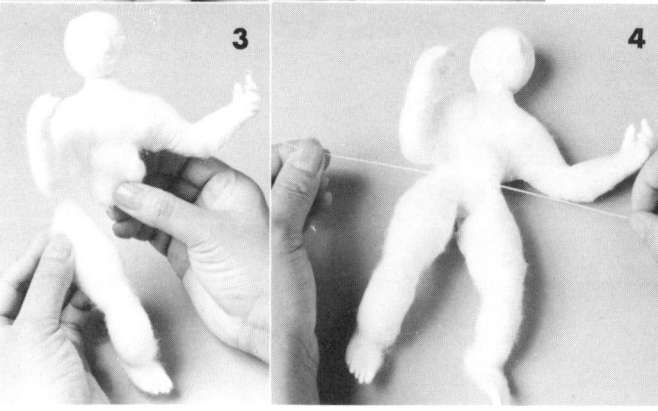

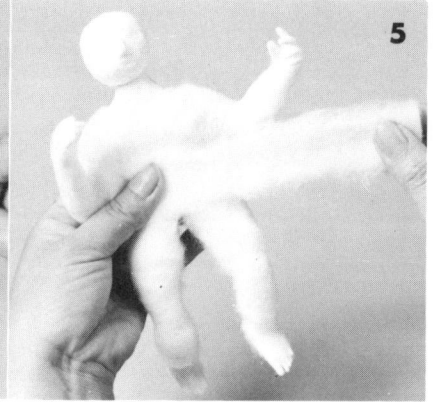

Stands (back cover) ━━━★

Materials
  Petals
   16 pieces of drawing paper for the backing (8.5×7 cm.)
   16 pieces of Japanese paper for the front and back (8.5×7 cm.)
   27 pieces of string (30 cm. long)

  Large stand
   2 pieces of corrugated cardboard for the backing of the top and bottom (10 cm. sq.)
   2 pieces of thick paper for the sides (30×1.5 cm.)
   2 pieces of paper for the top and bottom (10 cm. sq.)
   1 piece for the sides (32×35 cm.)

Small stand
- 2 pieces of corrugated cardboard for the top and bottom (8.5 cm. sq.)
- 2 pieces of thick paper for the sides (26.5×1 cm.)
- 2 pieces of paper for the top and bottom (8.5 cm. sq.)
- 1 piece for the sides (28.5×3 cm.)

How to Cut It Out
Use the pattern to cut out the backing for the petals. Do likewise with the paper for the front and back. Use the pattern to cut out the backing A and B for the tops and bottoms of the large and small stands. Cut two of each. Do likewise with backing C and D for the sides. Cut two of each out of the paper for the tops and bottoms. Do likewise for the sides, but make these pieces 1 cm. bigger all around.

How to Make It
Petals: Glue two pieces of the backing together for each petal. Glue on the string as shown in ①. Glue on the paper for the front and back. Cut off along the edge.
Large stand: Glue the backing for the sides to the paper for the sides. Overlap them a little and glue. Put glue on the edges of the paper. Put the backing for the bottom on top of the sides. Fold the edges of the paper for the sides over and glue to the backing. Turn it over and do the same with the backing for the top. Glue on the paper for the outside of the top and bottom. Do likewise with the small stand. Next, glue the petals on the large stand as shown in ③. Glue the small stand on top of the large one.

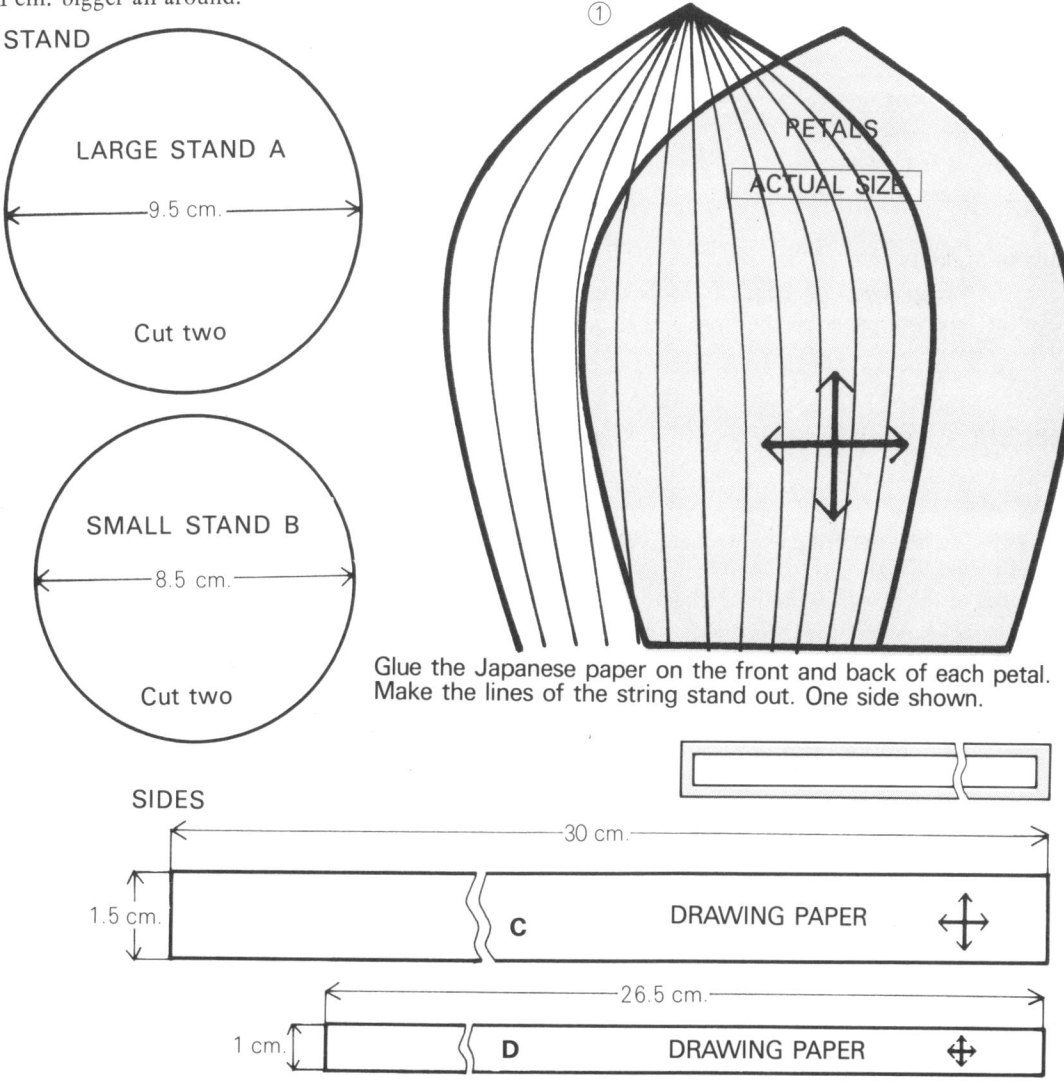

STAND

LARGE STAND A
9.5 cm.
Cut two

SMALL STAND B
8.5 cm.
Cut two

① PETALS ACTUAL SIZE

Glue the Japanese paper on the front and back of each petal. Make the lines of the string stand out. One side shown.

SIDES
30 cm.
1.5 cm.
C DRAWING PAPER

26.5 cm.
1 cm.
D DRAWING PAPER

79

② Two sides shown

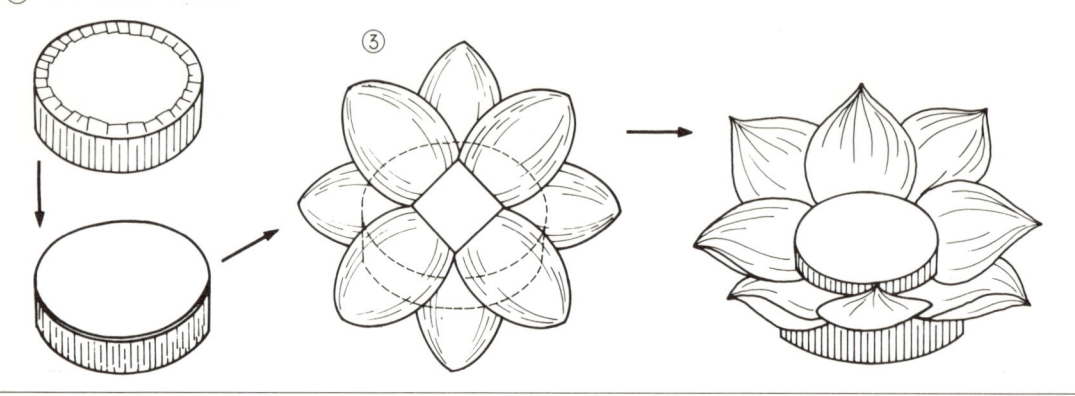

③

Crown (back cover) ━━━━━★

Materials
1 piece of drawing paper for the backing (5 cm. sq.)
2 pieces of Japanese paper with a gold print (5 cm. sq.)
1 piece of string.

How to Cut It Out
Use the pattern to cut out the backing.

How to Make It
Glue the string along the edge of the baking. Glue the Japanese paper on the front and back.

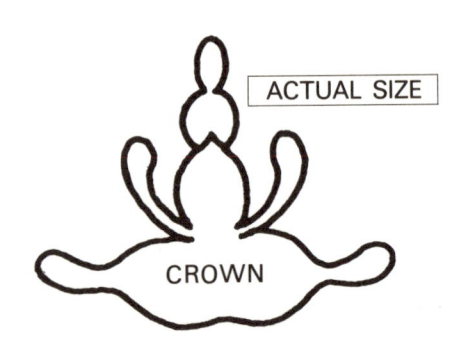

ACTUAL SIZE

CROWN

Make the line of the string stand out. Cut the Japanese paper off along the edge of the backing. Make a small necklace like the one you made before and put a ball in the center. Glue it on the crown.

Necklace (back cover) ━━━━━★

Materials
1 piece of Japanese paper (2 cm. × the length of the necklace).
1 piece of thick red decorative string.
2 pieces of Japanese paper for the flower (2 × 7 cm.)
An adequate amount of Japanese paper for the ball.
Cotton.

How to Make It
1. Put a little glue down the center as shown in sketch ①. Place it on a desk or table. Starting from one end, hold it down with the end of a pencil while holding it securely with tweezers. Repeat until it is the desired length.
2. Cut and glue the pieces of red string as shown in the sketch.

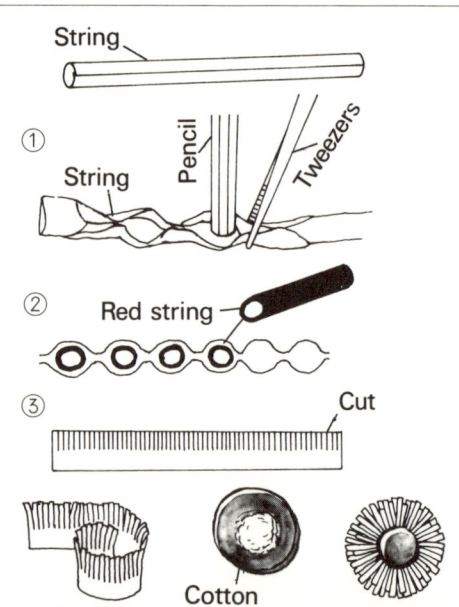

① String / Pencil / Tweezers / String

② Red string

③ Cut

Cotton

3. Make a flower and put it on where you joined both ends of the necklace. Glue the ball with cotton inside in the center of the flower.

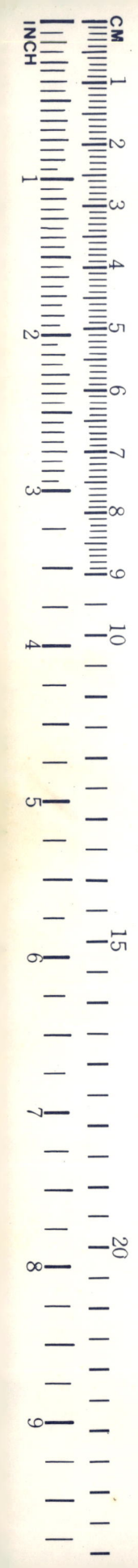